B.B.C. REFERENCE LIBRARY

This book should be returned on or before the last date stamped below.

16. ...
25. AUG 1993
-3. OCT 1993
24. ...

PLEASE RETURN BOOKS PERSONALLY OR BY LIBRARY MESSENGER RATHER THAN BY INTERNAL POST

A/259 11.76

BB 0205071 4

Problems of Contemporary French Politics

By the same author

THE FRENCH POLITICAL SCENE
FRANCE BETWEEN THE REPUBLICS
FRENCH POLITICS: THE FIRST YEARS OF THE
  FOURTH REPUBLIC
FRANCE: THE FOURTH REPUBLIC
ALGERIA AND FRANCE
INTRODUCTION TO POLITICS
THE FIFTH FRENCH REPUBLIC
FRANCE (Oxford Modern World Series)
THE UNEASY ENTENTE
DEMOCRACY
THE GOVERNMENT AND POLITICS OF FRANCE:
Volume I – Institutions and Parties
Volume II – Politics

DOROTHY PICKLES

Problems of Contemporary French Politics

METHUEN
LONDON AND NEW YORK

First published in 1982 by
Methuen & Co. Ltd
11 New Fetter Lane, London EC4P 4EE
Published in the USA by
Methuen & Co.
in association with Methuen, Inc.
733 Third Avenue, New York, NY 10017

© 1982 Dorothy Pickles

Photoset by Rowland Phototypesetting Ltd
Printed in Great Britain by
Richard Clay (The Chaucer Press) Ltd,
Bungay, Suffolk

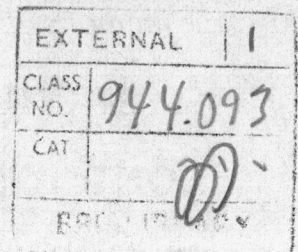

All rights reserved. No part of this book may
be reprinted or reproduced or utilized in any
form or by any electronic, mechanical or other
means, now known or hereafter invented,
including photocopying and recording, or in
any information storage or retrieval system, without
permission in writing from the publishers.

British Library Cataloguing in Publication Data
Pickles, Dorothy
Problems of contemporary French politics.
1. France—Politics and government—1958–
I. Title
944.083   DC417

ISBN 0 416 73230 5
ISBN 0 416 73240 2 Pbk

Library of Congress Cataloging in Publication Data
Pickles, Dorothy Maud.
Problems of contemporary French politics.
Includes bibliographical references and index.
1. France – Politics and government – 1969–
2. France – Foreign relations – 1969 3. France
  – Presidents.   I. Title.
DC421.P53   320.944   81-18804
ISBN 0 416 73230 5   AACR2
ISBN 0 416 73240 2 (pbk.)

For Judith
And for both of us
In memory of Bill

Contents

	Preface	ix
1	The significance of the Gaullist decade	1
2	The problem of electoralism	14
3	Problems of the left	27
4	Problems of the right	47
5	The decline of Gaullist foreign policy	68
6	Giscardian foreign policy problems: Europe	86
7	Giscardian foreign policy problems: defence	106
8	The perennial problem of the presidency	121
	Notes	146
	Index	155

Preface

This brief study of political problems during the years following the resignation and death of General de Gaulle is limited to three specific areas. The first is that of party-political and electoral controversy during twelve years dominated by elections and electoral speculation. Opposition and government parties confronted each other during this period in three presidential and three general elections and also in the first elections to the European Assembly. Though a period of political and economic change, it was one without any crisis or challenge such as the previous decade had seen in 1958, to a smaller degree in 1962 and again in 1968 with the student 'revolution'. It began in an atmosphere of relief at the achievement of the transition, after eleven years of the Gaullist presidency, to political life without de Gaulle, and ended with the creation of a totally new situation – the election of a Socialist President and a Socialist majority in the National Assembly, but in an atmosphere of pessimism, political disillusionment and party rivalries and dissensions.

The second area is that of foreign affairs, in which, despite the considerable degree of consensus that survives the transition to post-Gaullism, there were marked disagreements both between and within parties on specific policies, and an atmosphere in which the confidence generated by General de Gaulle's plans for France's future had already given way to disappointments regarding European plans and to anxieties regarding the future of east-west relations. It ended without any discernible improvement in the situation or in any significant changes in party attitudes to it.

The third area is an attempt to look at the presidency in the light of the concepts of three very different holders of the office within twelve years – Gaullism, followed by the Pompidolist variety of it, Giscardism and Socialism – to discuss the problems of the first two periods and to look forward to those that may be encountered during the third period.

It is always difficult to write on current French politics, and some of the views and tentative conclusions (where any are reached) will no doubt be contradicted by future unexpected events. There are bound to be errors of judgement, and perhaps also errors of fact. I am extremely grateful to Mr A. J. Woolmer and my daughter, Judith Louis, for undertaking the taxing work of reading the manuscript, and also to my son-in-law, Keith Louis, for reading the proofs. Their very useful comments, criticisms and suggestions have enabled me to correct some avoidable errors, obscurities or misleading statements. Those that no doubt remain are entirely my responsibility.

Since this is not a systematic study, but rather a commentary on current issues and opinions, no general bibliography is included. Notes are, however, provided, mainly in order that readers may judge for themselves how representative or convincing the opinions quoted seem to them to be. Those who feel the need of more factual background material than could be given within the scope of this study will no doubt consult two excellent books that have recently been published (both with comprehensive bibliographies): Vincent Wright's *Government and Politics of France* (1978) and J. R. Frears's *Political Parties and Elections in the Fifth French Republic* (1978).

DOROTHY PICKLES

Note: Chapter 5, 'The decline of Gaullist foreign policy', originally appeared in a slightly altered form in *International Affairs*, April 1975. The author and publishers would like to thank the Royal Institute of International Affairs for permission to reproduce this article. For this volume it has been brought up to date where necessary.

1 The significance of the Gaullist decade

When General de Gaulle became the twenty-first – and last – Prime Minister of the Fourth Republic in June 1958, few people in France, even among the relatively small band of his committed supporters, would have predicted with any confidence that he would be President of the Fifth Republic for more than a decade, that is, for a period only just over a year shorter than the entire life of the previous regime. At the end of that decade, many, including both supporters and opponents, were still far from confident that either the regime or the Gaullist party could survive without him.

In spite of the considerable powers attributed to the President under the new constitution, and of those assumed *de facto* by the first holder of the office, he remained for the first four years essentially at the mercy of circumstances. He was indispensable, but only so long as he was generally regarded as offering the only chance of obtaining a political solution of the Algerian problem (a military solution was by then out of the question). It had defeated the half-dozen Prime Ministers who had preceded him, brought down the regime, and created serious disaffection and unrest in the French army, most of which was, by then, in Algeria. But in what seemed at the time to be the unlikely event of his success in bringing the war to an end, he would, of course, immediately cease to be indispensable and so in all probability would be obliged to return to the political wilderness, as he had done in 1946 – with the difference that, though the constitution of the Fourth Republic was born and survived without him, that

2 Problems of Contemporary French Politics

of the Fifth (and especially the provisions relating to the power of the President) was generally regarded as being largely his creation, and so would have been unlikely to survive without him.

That he did succeed in bringing the Algerian war to an end, and also in surviving the ensuing political and constitutional challenge that he had accurately foreseen, was mainly due to his own skill in exploiting what assets he had, but also due in part to the lack of skill of the opposition parties in presenting themselves as credible alternatives. In the four successful referenda held during these years (in 1958, 1961, April and October 1962), whatever the question ostensibly put to the electors, they recognized that what they were being asked to decide was whether the President should remain in office on his own terms or resign and leave it to disunited and programmeless parties to provide a successor. The answers in each case were yes to de Gaulle, because he at least knew where he wanted to go and had the backing of a parliamentary majority in a National Assembly docile and disciplined enough to ensure that whatever Gaullist policies circumstances permitted could be implemented.

The fourth of these referenda, in October 1962, when the Algerian problem had been settled, asked the electorate to approve the President's proposed revision of the constitution to provide henceforth for presidential election by universal suffrage, instead of by the small electoral college of (mainly local) notabilities, which was the system originally provided in the 1958 constitution. Public opinion was divided on the issue, but the majority of Deputies in the National Assembly regarded the procedure of constitutional revision by referendum as being in itself unconstitutional and so defeated the Government – the only parliamentary defeat of the decade. This was the challenge that the President had expected, once the Algerian problem was out of the way. However, a majority still said yes to de Gaulle in the referendum, while the general election that followed increased the strength of the Gaullist party.

It was difficult to know how far these results were due to relief (and perhaps gratitude) for the settlement of the eight-year war, to fears that army unrest and the recent terrorist attacks in France indicated that the problem was not yet necessarily over, or to the popularity of the President's campaign in favour of the referendum as a truly democratic instrument of government. But the test clearly indicated that public opinion did not yet consider de Gaulle to be expendable.

He could, therefore, look forward with confidence to a period of prolonged political stability, once the remaining hurdle of his re-election for a second septennate had been surmounted in 1965.

That re-election also helped to strengthen the political authority of the President. The fact that his Socialist opponent (supported by Communist votes) acquiesced in the application of the new presidential electoral system that the opposition parties had opposed meant that this was now, in effect, 'constitutionalized', and so no longer a divisive political issue. Indeed, by 1965 opposition parties had come to recognize how vital a political asset a popularly elected President could be. Henceforth, arguments regarding the need to revise the constitution, that had hitherto largely dominated opposition political attitudes, played only a minor role. There was a general recognition that the Fifth Republic was there to stay.

By 1965 too the achievements of the regime helped to encourage this view. First, there was the demonstration of political and governmental stability – only two Prime Ministers in eight years, both Gaullists, as against the twenty governments and fifteen different Prime Ministers of differing political complexions during the Fourth Republic. Moreover, governments of the Fifth Republic were able to govern, thanks not only to greater political cohesion but also to parliamentary procedures designed by the makers of the new constitution to reduce parliamentary obstruction. Budgets were voted on time; deficits were eliminated; and the President's plan to modernize the French economy, reorganize and nuclearize the French army and restore French status in the world were visibly being systematically carried out.

The six years of Georges Pompidou's premiership from 1962 to 1968 saw the regular elaboration and application of successive five-year plans, worked out by co-operation between government departments, trade unions and industrial leaders, together with administrative reforms, including a comprehensive plan for regional economic institutions to be set up from 1964 onwards and – during the later years of the decade – increasing numbers of collective agreements in industry, including the introduction of some worker participation.

General de Gaulle was himself the most indefatigable propagandist for these achievements. He constantly held out to his compatriots the prospect of transforming France, often called in the 1950s 'the sick man of Europe', into a prosperous modern economy 'owing nothing to anybody'. By 1965 he could justifiably claim that in just over seven years five essential problems had been dealt with:

> Our institutions, which used to create impotence, are now replaced by a head of state, a government that lasts and governs, and a Parliament that carries out with dignity and efficiency its legislative functions. Decolonization, a subject that divided the French, alienated everyone else and disturbed our army, has now been achieved. Peace, which we have not known for at least half a century, has been recovered. Inflation, which undermined our economy, our finances and our currency, which maintained constant social insecurity and perpetual injustice, has now been checked. And finally, our independence has been regained, instead of being stifled by a mass of lying myths.[1]

In the field of foreign policy, the successful completion of decolonization in the early 1960s (by the accession to independence of twelve associated overseas states within a period of two years) certainly helped to increase France's standing in the Third World, where, in spite of the long drawn-out struggle over Algeria, France was regarded as a great decolonizer and also as a western power determined to stand up to the United States and to cultivate good relations with the Soviet Union. And although, outside France, the claim to 'independence' in the military field had no credibility, at least from 1965 onwards France had an operational, if small, nuclear force.

What the electorate appreciated more than anything else was the image deliberately built up by the President of a great country becoming herself again – no longer condemned to be 'a second-class nation'. The memories of war-time defeats and post-war humiliations were being wiped out by the comforting Gaullist myth of a 'European Europe' of which France was destined to be the leader, and of a regained 'national independence', due in part to developing nuclear power, but also to new-found economic prosperity and political stability, and perhaps above all to the Gaullist claim to a special French role in the world as the protagonist of a policy of 'détente and co-operation' with the Soviet Union and the eastern *bloc*. This last-mentioned role, popularized from 1963–4 onwards and emphasized during the 1965 election campaign for de Gaulle's re-election, was universally acceptable. Gaullists saw it as a demonstration of French status in the non-communist world. The left welcomed it for the essentially incompatible reason that Franco-Soviet *rapprochement* was a traditional part of left-wing ideology.

More important, however, it was seen by both right and left as an affirmation of a French role in the world demonstrably independent of the United States. Not only had France resented from the first the inevitable domination by the United States of the Atlantic alliance, but this resentment increased the strength of an anti-Americanism going back to the early post-war years. It was expressed by the left mainly in hostility to the American role in the Vietnam War, and to the activities of 'multinational' companies regarded as expressions of American domination. On the right, there was still resentment at what had been felt to be the exclusion of France from international conferences at Yalta and Potsdam. General de Gaulle himself, in the first posthumous volumes of his *Mémoires*, exhibited a quite surprising degree of animosity to American attitudes, and a leading French authority on French foreign policy described him as being in the 1960s 'obsessed by anti-Americanism'.[2]

The presidential contest in 1965, nevertheless, proved surprisingly – and for the government side uncomfortably – close. The President was obliged to play a much more active part in the campaign during the period between the two ballots in order to ensure his re-election. After a decade out of power, the opposition parties regarded 45.49 per cent of the votes as justifying the conclusion that a left-wing victory was now in sight. The result was that, for both sides, electoral preoccupations became increasingly dominant, and both sides proved unable to adapt themselves to the situation. The left's failure was predictable, given the fact that the Socialists could not hope to win a presidential election without massive support from the Communists, together with the votes of some Centrists. Yet any move towards either of these organizations risked alienating as many votes as it was likely to attract. The obvious results of this situation were perpetual wrangles, the fudging of issues, or both. And whatever electoral understanding was reached, the chances of its surviving the test of an attempt by Socialists and Communists to govern together were negligible.

On the government side, there was a similar need for understanding between Gaullists and the Conservative group that had governed in coalition with them since 1958, and also for some Centrist votes. On this side, too, there were tensions and disagreements. Gaullists faced the problem that, without the historical links of the traditional parties, their cohesion depended entirely on their allegiance to General de Gaulle, now an old man without any discernible dauphin. Indeed, to some Gaullists, the very idea of a successor appeared as some kind of treachery. And General de Gaulle himself remained firmly opposed to the transformation of a Gaullist movement, which was a national *rassemblement* held together only by loyalty to him, into an orthodox party with the machinery required in modern political systems to maintain cohesion and win elections.

This double party political stalemate continued to exist for the rest of the decade and beyond, with the result that there was in all parties a great deal of uncertainty regarding the political future. Some critics argued, indeed, that it might well prove impossible for the Gaullist party to survive without the leadership of the President and the discipline of power, and impossible for the opposition parties to maintain whatever cohesion had been reached in opposition if they were faced with the exigencies of power. The first test came with the general election of 1967, which proved a disappointment to both sides. Socialists and Communists fighting in general co-operation, if not in harmony, did not achieve their hoped-for majority, while the government parties were returned by the narrowest of majorities.

It was a measure of de Gaulle's success in focusing French politics entirely on himself that, while he alone appeared not to be thinking seriously of 'l'après-gaullisme', from 1965 onwards the political parties thought of practically nothing else. Nevertheless they were incapable of projecting their thought efficiently into a future of which he would not be a part. Statements made by prominent Gaullist personalities offered little comfort. 'The President of the Republic', wrote René Capitant in 1967, 'is not and must not become the head of a party or a super-party. . . . As long as de Gaulle is there we have nothing to fear; he will not allow himself to be imprisoned by any Parliamentary majority.'[3] But what was to happen when he was no longer there?

The question was answered – at least provisionally – sooner than most people had expected. Between 1968 and 1974 several significant changes combined to precipitate France into post-Gaullism.

Looked at with hindsight, the word 'happening' is perhaps the most accurate description of the first. In May 1968 disquiet and disruption in the university world, associated mainly with politically active left-wing student movements, suddenly erupted into a kind of bizarre mini-revolution, fuelled, after some initial hesitation, by trade union direct action, actually in support of wage claims rather than left-wing political objectives. After some three weeks of strikes and growing industrial as well as university chaos, the movement died down as suddenly as it had arisen. The trade unions negotiated a large wage increase, and so lost interest in the political angle; the general public lost interest in the students and went off in their thousands for the Whitsun holiday; and the political parties found themselves facing another general election, following the President's dissolution of the National Assembly. The result, thanks largely to some astute Gaullist tactics, was a landslide victory for the Government and the President.

The second change was that of the presidential image. General de Gaulle had been absent from France during the first week of May when the 'events' began, and his first public statement was not made until nearly three weeks later, when he broadcast a short appeal for support, promised (somewhat vaguely) structural reforms, and announced that the public would be consulted by 'the most direct and democratic method' – the referendum. The contrast between this broadcast and previous statements in times of crisis was striking. Writing of the Algerian insurrection in 1961, Jacques Fauvet had described him as being 'at his best in a storm. He seems almost to enjoy it, and it is a fact that it increases ten fold his capacities of manoeuvre and command. To those around him he appears unruffled.'[4]

In 1968, to most of those who heard him, he appeared both ruffled and uncertain of himself. In the circumstances, which he himself described as 'a tide of disorder, disruption and strikes', a referendum was obviously impractical, and nothing more was heard of the proposal. A week later, when he announced the dissolution of the National Assembly and appealed for support for the maintenance of the Republic in a general election, he seemed to have recovered his touch. Nevertheless, the man who now appeared to be really in charge – who negotiated a settlement with the unions and master-minded the Gaullist campaign in the election – was not the President, but the Prime Minister. In the reshuffle following the Gaullist victory, Pompidou found himself, however, replaced as Prime Minister by the definitely non-charismatic Finance Minister and former Minister of Foreign Affairs, Maurice Couve de Murville. Henceforth relegated to the back benches, Pompidou became an available, acceptable and, when the time came, willing, potential presidential candidate at large. The question: after de Gaulle, who? was no longer unanswerable.

The third event came as the result of a presidential miscalculation. In April 1969, he submitted to a referendum (his fifth) two measures that the electorate were asked to approve by a single yes or no, with the normal understanding that if a majority voted no, the President would not remain in office. One of the measures, proposing regional reforms, was in principle popular. The other was an unpopular plan to reform the Senate along functional lines. This was an old plan of de Gaulle's, outlined by him as far back as 1946, in a speech known as 'the Bayeux constitution'. For the first and last time, therefore, the majority said no to de Gaulle. He forthwith resigned.

As a loyal and capable Prime Minister of de Gaulle for six years, widely regarded as the chief architect of the Gaullist victory in the general election of 1968, Pompidou was the obvious favourite in the following presidential election and, on 19 June, became the second President of the Fifth Republic.

The Pompidolist interlude

The smoothness of the transition from Gaullism to what was not yet post-Gaullism, but what the Gaullist old guard called *Pompidolisme*, was no doubt in part due to fears of a recurrence of the political and social disturbance of 1968, and to still fresh memories of the role played by Pompidou in dealing with them. It was also in part due to his own tactics and to his personal qualities. His campaign was based on the slogan 'Continuity and Change', with the emphasis understandably on the first, since, though he was known to have ideas of his own both regarding the organization of the party and in foreign affairs, he was bound to be inhibited by the brooding and silent presence of his predecessor in retirement in Colombey-les-deux-Eglises. Indeed, he was reported to have admitted in private that he felt constrained by 'le poids de ses silences'. His freedom of action was also inhibited by critics in the Gaullist party, especially by fundamentalist leaders such as Michel Debré, who did not want *any* change, and by the more progressive elements among, for instance, the *Gaullistes de gauche*, who feared that there might be too few changes, and that some Gaullist reforms, especially that of worker participation, might be slowed down or dropped. In any case, whatever the new President's own views, he could not afford to make any spectacular departure from policies that he had advocated and applied during the previous six years of his premiership.

As things turned out, a number of factors combined to make his presidency a brief interlude rather than a definitive transition. The sudden death of de Gaulle in November 1970 might have allowed him to make his own personality and politics more fully felt if it had not been for two obstacles, the changes in the political climate and his rapidly failing health. Though both his presidential and his oratorical style differed greatly from those of de Gaulle, he was an eloquent and elegant speaker, an intelligent communicator and a competent and authoritative head of the executive. He certainly managed to negotiate with skill British entry into the EEC on conditions satisfactory to the French public. And he followed up efforts made by General de Gaulle to extend the activities of the EEC into the political field with political initiatives of his own, though without success. But, by 1973, criticisms of his leadership, or more exactly of his failure to provide leadership and decision, were becoming more frequent, and in the following year it had become no longer possible to hide from the public the truth about his physical condition. In the spring of 1974, he died.

His most significant political achievement was undoubtedly to maintain the regime intact through the necessarily difficult period of transition from the peculiarly personal conception of the de Gaulle presidency to a form of Gaullism without de Gaulle – that is, essentially, from government by charisma to government by persuasion. Many Gaullists had feared that this transition might prove impossible. Some appeared to resent it, But what was baptized *Pompidolisme* was inevitably a holding operation. There was no clear evidence that, even if Pompidou had not had to contend with ill-health as well as with economic difficulties and foreign policy frustrations, he could have provided overall objectives of his own that would have been capable of attracting the kind of public support that the Gaullist Grand Design had obtained. For one thing, the 1970s were to prove a different world, and for another his background and personality were perhaps more those of a second-in-command than a leader. Moreover, he lacked the most essential asset of all – he was not indispensable.

As it turned out, his capacities were not put to the test. The real problems affecting the future of the Gaullist regime were therefore deferred until the presidency of his successor. Valéry Giscard d'Estaing had served as Finance Minister in all Gaullist governments from 1962–6, and again throughout Pompidou's presidency. He was not a Gaullist and did not become one, and so he lacked some advantages from the start. He was not wholly acceptable to the Gaullist party, and the party of which he was the leader was the minority partner in the government coalition. For almost two years, however, he did not appear to encounter any serious difficulties. He chose as his Prime Minister a young Gaullist, Jacques Chirac, a protégé of Pompidou, who, during the election campaign, deserted the official Gaullist candidate and former Prime Minister, Jacques Chaban-Delmas, taking some forty or more Gaullist politicians with him, thus greatly contributing to Giscard d'Estaing's victory. The Gaullist party still dominated the National Assembly, its strength having been first reduced in the 1967 election, then greatly increased by the landslide victory in the general election that had followed the 'May events' of 1968, and finally consolidated at a somewhat more modest level in the 1973 elections. The President's foreign policy appeared to be in conformity with the existing pattern, in that he clearly accepted the Gaullist interpretation of 'national independence' as requiring the continued absence of France from NATO and in that he sought, by his European initiatives, to achieve his predecessors' aims of increasing France's political weight in Europe and of resisting any proposals for changes in the Rome treaty, and especially in the Common Agricultural Policy, finally completed only in 1970.

By the summer of 1976, however, it was clear to all that there were serious differences between the President and his Prime Minister. After some weeks of widespread rumours, Chirac resigned on 25 August. The composition of the new Government revealed few changes – a slight increase in the proportion of Ministers declaring themselves to be 'Presidentialists', an additional Minister representing the left-centre, and a triumvirate of senior Ministers, promoted to the position of *Ministres d'Etat*, and representing respectively the Gaullist, Independent Republican, and centre elements in the government coalition. The one significant change was the appointment as Prime Minister of the professional economist, Raymond Barre, who was intended to be, and proved to be, a loyal Giscardian. For the first time in eighteen years, France had neither a Gaullist President nor a Gaullist Prime Minister.

The 1976 government, therefore, clearly marks the real beginning of the post-Gaullist era, which was to have its own political problems, different in many ways from those of the 1960s and likely to prove more intractable. Indeed, it could fairly be said that, politically, from 1976 onwards the President was increasingly facing apparently insoluble problems. The Gaullist era had been dominated by three main issues: first, Algeria and decolonization; second, during the middle years, by foreign policy and defence, and especially the problems involved in establishing a working European Economic Community incorporating the policies of the Common Agricultural Policy, in achieving the French withdrawal from NATO, and in providing France with a national nuclear deterrent; third, during the last years, the main concerns had been in the administrative field, including educational reform (after the disruption of the universities in 1968) as well as the establishment and organization of the system of regional administrative bodies provided for by the 1964 reforms.

None of these played any significant part in the political problems that mainly preoccupied governments and electors in the first post-Gaullist decade. But no less important than the problems themselves were the changes in the political and economic climate and their impact on governments. In contrast to General de Gaulle, who was regarded as being in some respects above the political battle, Giscard d'Estaing appeared less remote. He was the admitted leader of a political party, whereas although Gaullists claimed they followed General de Gaulle's leadership, he himself always refused the title of leader of any party, even the Gaullist party. President Giscard d'Estaing was inevitably involved in the party battle, and vulnerable to attacks from the dominant party in his government coalition. Nor did he have the advantages enjoyed by General de Gaulle of an economic climate of increasing prosperity. The oil crisis had already become a problem before he became President. And he inherited a number of problems and difficulties, which made the satisfaction of French hopes and expectations more problematical.

It is not possible, within the scope of this short study, to do more than discuss briefly, and inevitably inadequately, a few of the specific problems that constituted the dominant political interests of political parties in the 1970s. Under the de Gaulle presidency, the political debate had been concerned with France's foreign policies in Europe and the world, with what was and ought to be the role of the President, with the relations between parties (and especially between Socialists and Communists), and, towards the end of the decade, increasingly with what the future would be after de Gaulle. In the following decade the main interest in internal politics was concentrated on party disagreements and election prospects, and the following chapters discuss three aspects of the subject: the obsession with electoral attitudes and opinion polls, the relations between Socialist and Communist parties on the opposition side, and between Gaullists and 'Giscardians' on the Government side. In the field of foreign policy, three specific problems are looked at: first, what has been called the decline of Gaullist foreign policy, by which is meant not so much the failure to attain the objectives proclaimed by General de Gaulle as the increasing difficulties in the 1970s of discovering ways in which France could even attempt to play the kind of role that Gaullists had seen as desirable and possible; second, the evolution of opinions regarding the future of the European Community; and, third, the increasing problems in the field of defence. The final chapter looks at the perennial problem of what the French believe that the role of the President is or ought to be.

Strictly speaking, although the President and the office of the presidency were much discussed during the 1960s, the subject was not in the forefront of discussion until the final years of the Giscardian septennate, and there was little apparent interest on the part of the public in the institutional aspects that had occupied a large place in debates during the de Gaulle presidency, especially in parties on the left. This was mainly due to the fact that by then there was in all parties a conviction that the 1962 reform had helped to transform the presidency into the supreme objective of all parties, and so none was prepared to forgo the power and influence that it conferred on the holder of the office and the parties supporting him. It might be said that the presidency remained throughout the decade a potential problem, in that it was capable at any time of arousing political discontent or personal criticism, but did not give rise to any positive proposals for change. In other words, perhaps it ought to have been more of a problem than in fact it was.

The treatment of these subjects within the framework of the present study is necessarily slight and inconclusive, since it seeks primarily to pinpoint the main emphases of party debates and dissensions, and the reactions of party leaders or potential party leaders to changes in the political situation and to changes in party prospects. What did seem to emerge during the course of the decade was a growing sense of political disillusionment among the rank and file of parties, a consciousness, not always very precise, that parties were increasingly out of touch with their rank and file, and that the latter were also increasingly out of touch with opinion outside the ranks of the parties. The expression 'la crise de régime' was heard more frequently than it had been since the years immediately preceding the fall of the Fourth Republic. Not that there seemed to be any precise fear of an impending danger to the regime. There was rather a sense of generalized political malaise, in part no doubt due to the growing realization of serious unresolved problems, to some sense of a loss of direction or of purpose since the death of de Gaulle, and to a growing realization of the inherent dangers of a political atmosphere of disillusionment with politicians and politics. Political memories in France are long, and everyone is aware of the speed with which, in the past, discontent has escalated into crisis, as it did, for instance, in 1958 and 1968.

For twenty-three years, however, the Fifth Republic has not fulfilled recurrent pessimistic predictions regarding its future. What the 1980s will bring is still anybody's guess.

2 The problem of electoralism

On 14 June 1978, President Giscard d'Estaing described France as having been involved in 'a more or less permanent electoral campaign ever since 1973'. The remark was equally applicable in 1980, and even more so in 1981, although the official presidential election campaign did not open until April. By the end of 1980, two of the main front runners had not yet confirmed their intention to stand, but a great many improbable candidates had presented themselves. For most of these, the declaration of candidature was no more than a political gesture or a search for publicity, and it was generally assumed that they would all drop out before the contest, either owing to lack of political or financial support, or through failure to comply with the legal requirements governing candidates for the presidency, especially those relating to sponsorship and deposit.

Public interest in the contest never flagged during these years. Indeed, to judge by the space given in the press to articles, reports of party conferences and television appearances of political personalities, it rose in a steady crescendo until, some months before the actual election, it seemed that everything that could possibly be said about the event and the personalities likely to be involved had already been said a hundred times over. Yet the flood of public opinion polls reported on regularly in the press were, it was alleged, only 'the tip of the iceberg'. The *sondage* had now become an event in itself. Jean Stoetzel, the creator of the IFOP opinion poll, even described 'political *sondages*' as having become 'more than an institution, a sort of fact of nature'.[1]

The development of electoralism

A notable characteristic of this permanent election fever was the extent to which political events, even when relatively unimportant, such as by-elections, or local election results, or statements by politicians in routine speeches, were dragged into the presidential speculation and used, or misused, to suggest the possible effects that they might have on the election scenario. Since both the Third and Fourth Republics had been accustomed to frequent elections, and, for the first fifteen years of the Fifth, four out of every five years were election years (if local, departmental and senatorial elections are included), it may be wondered why the decade of the 1970s was characterized by 'electoralism' to the extent that it was. One reason may have been that the election of the two previous Presidents came unexpectedly and so there was no long period during which pre-electoral speculation could develop. The presidential election of 1969 followed General de Gaulle's resignation and that of Giscard d'Estaing in 1974 followed on the death of Pompidou. General de Gaulle's election for a second term in 1965 was certainly preceded by a couple of years of speculation and party manoeuvring, but without all the paraphernalia of the involvement of the mass media.

There would seem to be two major features in the development of the electoralism of the 1970s. The first was the effect on electoral behaviour of the changes in the relationship between the two main parties making up, respectively, the government and opposition coalitions. Between 1967 and 1978, the Gaullist party, which had remained dominant in government and in a majority in the National Assembly, lost its commanding position. In 1970, the Gaullist writer, Jean Charlot, had gone as far as to predict that the dominance of Gaullism would become a permanent characteristic of French politics.[2] In the 1973 election, however, although the government coalition retained the majority of seats in the National Assembly, the Gaullist party lost nearly 100 seats. In the 1978 election, it no longer retained its dominant position within the government coalition. The newly created 'Giscardian' UDF (*Union pour la démocratie française*) came within twenty votes of the Gaullists, who won 57 of their 153 seats by majorities of under 1 per cent.

In 1976, a new relationship within the coalition had been created when the Gaullist Prime Minister, Jacques Chirac, resigned. Up to then, though the theory that President and Prime Minister were politically (if not constitutionally) bound to agree had not been directly challenged, this was only because, when serious disagreements did arise, it was always the Prime Minister who gave way. Thus, Debré resigned in 1962, clearly in deference to the President's views, Pompidou's resignation was requested by General de Gaulle in 1968, and, in 1972, when he himself was President, he had obtained the resignation of his own Prime Minister. Since all those involved were Gaullists the resignations had taken place without any friction, and a discreet silence was kept regarding the reasons for them. In 1976, there was a non-Gaullist President, Giscard d'Estaing, and a Gaullist Prime Minister who did not keep a discreet silence, but publicized the reasons for his resignation. From then on, it became progressively more evident that frictions existed between the two major partners in the government coalition.

During the presidential election campaign of 1974 there had been, it is true, rival government candidates at the first ballot (Giscard d'Estaing and Chaban-Delmas), but both had fought a restrained campaign, well aware that the loser's supporters would be asked to cast their votes for his opponent at the second ballot, since their common opponent was the Socialist candidate. By the end of 1980, after some years of increasingly active criticism of the President by Gaullist members of the government coalition in the National Assembly, there were already three declared Gaullist candidates prepared to oppose the 'Giscardian' candidate (universally expected to be the President himself). Moreover, the Gaullist party had been weakened since the death of de Gaulle by the existence of different strands of opinion within the party and by the failure of any party leader to emerge who could claim the support of the whole party. The Giscardians, however, had succeeded by then in including their disparate elements in a single federation, which, thanks largely to the prestige of its association with the President, who was its *de facto* though not its *de jure* leader, had created a strong and much better organized electoral machine than had been at the disposal of the former *Républicains indépendants*.

On the opposition side, things had changed too. In 1972, after years of argument, Socialists and Communists had formed an electoral alliance on the basis of a common government programme, though both parties also retained their separate party programmes alongside this, thus creating a situation not without ambiguity. This alliance enabled the party to improve the situation of the left in the 1973 election, but though the left obtained a majority of the votes cast, the government coalition still retained the majority of the seats. In the 1974 presidential election, the Socialist leader, Mitterrand, standing as a united left candidate against a visibly divided right, obtained 43.97 per cent of the votes at the first ballot, and came within half a million votes of those cast for Giscard d'Estaing at the second ballot – within sight of a left victory, if the two parties could remain united on the basis of the 1972 alliance. In the event, however, they were unable to do this, and after three years of increasingly acrimonious argument, the break came in 1977, from which point the Communist party appeared to devote its entire energies to attacking the Socialist party. Both party leaders defended what, to a British observer, seemed at first sight a ridiculous as well as an implausible position, claiming to be in favour of the Union of the Left, which each accused the other of having betrayed. The explanation was in fact simple, though not for that reason any less potentially electorally damaging. Both suspected their own rank and file of being in favour of union (since the eternal illusion of the left has been that, somehow, it must be possible for Communists and Socialists to find a basis for jointly opposing and eventually defeating the right). But one lesson that the experiment of the Common Programme had taught both partners was that co-operation served mainly the interests of the stronger partner. The aim, therefore, of both parties became quite openly to demonstrate its own superiority in whatever electoral contest took place.

This change in party relations was not so much a return to the four 'political families', into which politicians like Guy Mollet and François Mitterrand had divided parties in France, as to a relationship that has been called 'a bi-polar quadrille', since, between the two partners in each coalition, boundaries were less clearly defined than they had been traditionally. In some ways, and especially on foreign policy issues, Communists and Gaullists had more in common with each other than each had with its ostensible ally. For both shared the Gaullist conception of nationalism and hostility to anything in the way of supranational or integrated control of defence. Giscardians and Socialists were nearer to each other in their vague 'Europeanism' in general and their lip-service to the idea of European integration.

Within each coalition, too, one partner was essentially intransigent, unable or unwilling to reach policy compromises, because party policies were derived from principles laid down in the one case by a dead leader and in the other by a foreign power – the Soviet Union.

The problem of Soviet control of the French Communist party had not previously been acute, because the French Communist party had been persistently in opposition since 1947. But its decision to abandon what was described as its 'ghetto' and form an alliance with the Socialist party based on a government programme raised immediately the problem of how the Socialist party and supporters of the alliance were to be convinced that the Communists had really had a change of heart. This problem is discussed in more detail in the following chapter. It is sufficient to say here that when the agreement finally broke down in 1977, it was hardly reassuring to Socialists who had been convinced – or had convinced themselves – that the Communists had changed to discover that the publicized changes – regarding Communist doctrine, regarding what was described as 'Eurocommunism' and independence of Moscow – all vanished overnight from Communist propaganda.

Undoubtedly, however, the major factor in encouraging electorialist exploitation of these changed relationships between parties was the actual working of the 1962 electoral law governing the election of the President. The closer-run the contest became, the more essential it became for each party to ensure that its own candidate secured the immense advantage of winning the presidential election, and as a first objective that its own candidate should be one of the two heading the poll at the first ballot. For the law laid down that only these two were eligible to stand a fortnight later for the second ballot which finally decided the issue.

It had been hoped by some political scientists that this provision in the act might encourage sufficient 'bi-polarization' to produce somewhat more coherent electoral alternatives. In the event, it greatly complicated electoral tactics, because electors who would be compelled to vote on the same side in the second ballot, in order to prevent the victory of the opposing coalition, would often have been opponents at the first. For some parties, in particular the Communist party, since the experience of Union of the Left, the important ballot was the first, which the party hoped to use to demonstrate the numerical superiority of the Communist over the Socialist party. For the Socialist party it was, however, equally necessary to demonstrate that the Socialists would be the major partner in any electoral alliance. These conflicting electoral preoccupations came to dominate the pre-campaign discussions to a point where it appeared impossible that any real attention would be paid to the presidential policies for which the electors were ostensibly voting.

Presidential policies were, moreover, in themselves productive of difficulties for the electors. For a presidential election risked producing conflicting national verdicts, in the absence of any institutional procedure to resolve the conflict. There was no necessary connection between the result of what was, in effect, a national referendum to elect a President, and the result of a national consultation in a general election which might be carried out at a different time, on different issues, and which employed a quite different procedure. The general assumption under the Fifth Republic was that the President was *de facto* head of the Government by virtue of his election by the whole nation, but the President was *de jure* dependent on the parliamentary majority's consent in order to permit the implementation of any policies put forward by him that required legislation. In the event of a clash between President and National Assembly, the only way out was for the President either to give way or to dissolve the National Assembly and hold fresh elections. If the result was then to recreate the deadlock, he would either have to give way or to resign and thus make a fresh presidential election necessary. For the National Assembly could constitutionally be dissolved by the President only once in twelve months. The electoral calculations and risks involved if these particular institutional provisions had to be applied – the need for which was described by Chaban-Delmas as the constitution's 'Achilles heel'[3] – were, of course, accompanied by serious political risks that nobody was anxious to take in the difficult circumstances of the 1970s. Except, perhaps, the Communist party, which might hope to derive advantage from political instability.

The problems of electoralism

If such a background perhaps makes the development of electoralism to the point that it had reached by the time of the election more comprehensible, it does not prevent it from possibly creating serious political problems. The kind of political problem that could arise is possibly best illustrated by quoting some examples of the lengths to which electoralism was taken. The examples are numerous and only a few can usefully be quoted here. For one thing, the very word became an accusation in itself, applied indiscriminately by one party or one individual to another, with the result that it was universally condemned yet appeared to be universally practised.

Examples of electoralism, though numerous, fall in practice into one of several categories. There were, to begin with, the obvious 'red herrings' – scandalmongering concerning individuals or parties, the purpose of which was usually to damage the image of the party involved or sometimes that of the President himself. The best known of these was the rumour circulated in 1979 and 1980 – at first in a well-known left-wing weekly – concerning an alleged gift of diamonds made to the President in 1973, when he was Minister of Finance, by the ruler of the Central African Republic. The press gave some prominence to the report and to the published facsimile of the letter from President Bokassa (as he was then); the Elysée services issued a formal denial of anything irregular, but the so-called *affaire* rumbled on in both the French and foreign press for some time, bringing in secondary personalities, charges and denials, including a television programme in which Michel Poniatowski, a former prominent member of the President's party, defended the President against damaging rumours and attacks of this kind. The possible damage was, of course, that of impugning the credibility of a government at a time when it was already coming under severe political criticism. At about the same time, the suicide of a former Minister led to rumours of his involvement in shady property transactions.

A few days earlier, a suggestion by the President that the Minister of Labour, together with the Minister for Industry, might do well to take into consideration recent proposals made by the trade union leader, Edmond Maire, with a view to introducing legislation designed to improve industrial relations, was immediately seized on by the Communist paper *l'Humanité* in order to accuse the two men of complicity in a 'political operation intended to prepare the way for a social consensus'. The accusation – or innuendo – by the Communist party spokesmen that either the Socialist party or the 'Giscardians' were seeking some secret understanding was, indeed, frequently made – sometimes, too, Socialist-Gaullist complicity was alleged –

the aim being to support the familiar Communist line that only the Communist party could be trusted to defend the workers' interests and to provide the party leader, Marchais, with opportunities to say over and over again 'non, non et non au consensus'.[4]

There were also, of course, less serious allegations or insinuations, generally aimed merely at politically discrediting or belittling the President or potential candidates – the criticism, for instance, that the President's foreign visits were 'a systematic electoral investment' or 'an electoralist manoeuvre';[5] the rumours (given extensive publicity) that there was something discreditable in the Communist leader's war-time life that both he and the Communist party were anxious to hide.[6] Such rumours, some more damaging, were fairly common in France, and the Gaullist decade had had its share of *affaires* that, as was usual, were never satisfactorily cleared up. But what characterized those concerned with electoral propaganda in the late 1970s was their number, often their triviality, and the sheer length of time during which they apparently successfully diverted attention from real political issues.

Two examples are, perhaps, worth quoting in some detail as illustrating first the extent of the electoralist obsession, and second the complexity of the actual or suspected tactical manoeuvres and counter-manoeuvres. The first was the conduct of the French campaign in 1979 to elect members to the European Assembly. It was extensively covered in the French political press, though readers could have been forgiven for not realizing from the press reports that the election concerned the functioning of a European institution and not that of the French Government (except for some characteristically nationalist speeches from Debré opposing the acquisition by the European Assembly of any legislative powers). The Socialist leader called on the electorate to vote against the present French Government's policy. 'Votes cast for Madame Veil' (the leader of the Giscardian list), he said, would be 'an encouragement to the policy of M. Raymond Barre.'[7] Jacques Chirac, leader of the Gaullist list, treated the election as a French anti-government referendum in the hope that it would be a kind of censure vote damaging to the Prime Minister – though he hoped not to the point of bringing the Government down.[8] André Laurens of *Le Monde* predicted at the beginning of May – a few weeks before the election – that the common denominator of the Gaullist and opposition parties on election day would be the French Prime Minister's economic and social policy.[9] Interviewed on 1 June, Mitterrand was asked whether the principal issue of the European election was not preparation for the French presidential election. He replied that it *was* for Madame Simone Veil.[10] In reality, however, Madame Veil did pay some attention to European issues, at least to the extent of pointing out the advantages to France of EEC policies.

Summing up the campaign after the election was over, Alain Duhamel reported in *Le Monde* that the Communist campaign had been 'wholly nationalist, negative and academic',[11] that most of it had been devoted to attacking the French Socialist party, and that the party's main interest had been to secure a higher poll than the Socialists, while the UDF objective had been to secure a higher poll than the Gaullists. Jean Rey (Socialist) described French political life as being wholly dominated by the presidential election,[12] and André Fontaine contributed to this concentration on French party-political issues by noting that Chirac's 'score', as he called it, had been only 1 per cent higher than that of his fellow-Gaullist Chaban-Delmas in the first ballot of the French presidential election of 1974.[13] For the Communist party, too, this purely national comparison was valid, and the Communist party noted with satisfaction that its vote in the European election had shown no decline compared with that obtained by the party in the French general election of March 1978. The most significant exhibition of French nationalist electoral obsession, however, was provided by the left-wing paper *Le Matin-Dimanche* on election day, which published a banner headline, stating simply:

PS et RPR en baisse.
UDF et PC en hausse.

What ought, perhaps, to have been the most significant statistic, but clearly was not, was the revelation that 39 per cent of French voters had not even bothered to vote.

The second example refers merely to one brief item of propaganda and the series of complex, interpretative speculations to which it gave rise. On 26 January 1981, a Communist spokesman accused Mitterrand of seeking some form of co-operation between Socialists and Giscardians in the event of the election of Giscard d'Estaing. At the same time he claimed in advance a number of ministerial posts for

Communists in the event of a victory for the Socialist candidate in the presidential election. The statement came as something of a surprise, since it had been expected that the Communist leader, Georges Marchais, would not raise the second point until much later. Whoever was to win the election, there would normally be no prospect of a change of government, for the existing Giscardian-Gaullist majority in the National Assembly was not due to face a general election until 1983. Moreover, the Communist statement in itself makes no obvious sense. Why should Communists want to co-operate with Socialists whom they were perpetually accusing of making overtures to the right?

The answer is, of course, that the Communist party had to work out its tactics in three distinct circumstances – before the first ballot, before the second ballot and after the election, if it should happen that a Socialist President would have to hold office with a right-wing majority continuing in Parliament.

The Communist move was interpreted as having two specific objectives. From the Communist point of view, the recent improvement reported by opinion polls of Mitterrand's chances made it appear more likely that he might be elected on the first ballot, thus defeating what was the primary aim of the Communist party, namely the demonstration that at the first ballot the Communist party could obtain more votes than the Socialists. A renewal of the accusation that the Socialist party was making overtures to the Giscardians was likely to deter some of his possible supporters from voting for him, while the suggestion that a Socialist President would include Communist Ministers in a left-wing government would no doubt deter some non-Socialists from voting for him, in preference to a Giscardian. This had certainly been the conclusion at the time of the 1974 presidential election, when Giscard d'Estaing, as a candidate, had asked Mitterrand some pertinent questions on the point. The Communist party also had another problem. It was feared that the prospect of a Socialist victory might lead some Communists to make sure of this by voting for the Socialist candidate at the *first* ballot, instead of waiting for the second, when the Communists would no doubt follow the traditional procedure of standing down for the left-wing victor of the first ballot. This, again, would defeat the Communists' aim of polling their full strength at the first ballot in order to assert their numerical superiority. Mitterrand had, in fact, stated (on 26 January 1980) that in the event of his election he would use his presidential power to dissolve the National Assembly and hold an immediate general election in the hope of obtaining a left-wing victory. He had done this, in part, precisely in order to ward off Communist suggestions that he would seek an understanding with the right in order to make it possible for President and Parliament to live together. This preventive announcement was now seen not to be effective.

The Socialists hoped to counter this latest Communist move by emphasizing in their campaign the specifically socialist elements of their own programme and by side-stepping the problem of possible Communist Ministers. They waited to see exactly how much disarray in the government camp would be created by differences between Chirac's and Giscard's supporters which might strengthen Mitterrand's bargaining position, and in the meantime they emphasized the adequacy of Mitterrand's own team of advisers.

How much of this type of electoral speculation and tactical warfare really appealed to electors was increasingly open to question as the long pre-campaign dragged on. But it must have suggested to many French voters, as well as to foreign observers of French politics, the political problems that party habits in conjunction with the working of the 1962 electoral law were helping to create. First, by concentrating so consistently and for so long on the negative operation of combating each other, parties were sacrificing consideration of electoral policies to scoring points against each other, and, moreover, against those who would be their government or opposition partners more than against their opponents. It was going to be all the more difficult for government coalitions to function when they had had their weak points publicized continuously for years rather than months. In fact, of course, matters of policy had been consistently ignored, and the political press, which normally provides both information and political debate, had filled its columns instead with speculations and often irrelevant and sometimes baseless attacks.

Inevitably, this process had led to a lowering of the whole tone of political controversy, as was seen in the numerous *affaires*, political and personal attacks, and rumours of misconduct of different kinds. Because the presidential election afforded such opportunities for press or radio publicity, it also attracted numbers of irresponsible, freak and minority candidatures – upwards of fifty or more eventually. This had always been a feature of French general elections, but for a much shorter period and involving far fewer cases. The most striking example of the deterioration in the quality of political debate was the attention paid to what ought to have been considered merely as an example of the familiar 'freak' candidature, namely that of a well-known music-hall clown, known as Coluche, whose sole apparent purpose in standing was to obtain publicity, and whose appeal consisted of abuse of all parties expressed in the colourful, vulgar, bawdy and sometimes scatological language familiar in his act.

Inevitably, too, some of the consequences of electoralism affected the presidency itself. President Giscard d'Estaing had visibly sought to appear as much 'above the battle' as was possible for someone more politically committed than General de Gaulle had been. Since his office was elective, he could not expect opponents to forego the right to make him a target of their criticism, just as supporters used him as an aid in their own cause. But he might well feel, as many Frenchmen must no doubt have felt, that he had the right to be immune from the kind of personal innuendo and attack that he suffered in the Bokassa affair, to which he could not reply without, by so doing, prolonging the painful publicity.[14] There is, of course, a law in France protecting the President of the Republic from personal attack and both General de Gaulle and Pompidou had recourse to it. But perhaps because the President was now elected by the nation, Giscard d'Estaing did not choose to do so.[15]

It is easy for British critics, accustomed to effective two-party systems in which there was a considerable element of bipartisan politics, to be critical of the electoralism of the Fifth Republic. Britain was fortunate in being able to maintain stable two-party parliamentary government for so long, and to avoid the kind of insoluble and divisive problem that Algeria had constituted for the Fourth Republic and Ireland for Great Britain in the 1970s. Electoralism was essentially a response to a party system, described by one writer as 'four characters in search of an author', but more accurately, perhaps, described as two couples unable to get on with each other or to change partners. The long process of finding a cure could be expensive – involving neglect of policies (the conspiracy of silence over defence problems for instance), the boredom or disaffection of the public, and the waste of presidential time in electioneering visits and broadcasts. Perhaps the most obvious first step might be to change the existing system of presidential election. Its introduction was preceded by a great deal of party controversy. It is ironic that two decades later a proposal to change it might well encounter opposition from all parties, united for once in the desire to retain it.

3 Problems of the left

The background

Since the formation of the Third Republic, the essential problem of parliamentary government in France has been that party and electoral systems have militated against the formation of stable majorities able to maintain stable governments. Under the Third Republic, numerous parties, for the most part loosely organized, and sometimes ephemeral, formed and reformed shifting majorities, a process encouraged by the institution of a virtually fixed tenure for Parliaments, together with what turned out in practice to be the absence of a safety-valve of dissolution. Under the Fourth Republic, the problem was complicated mainly by two factors. First, though strong and disciplined parties had grown up on the left, Socialists and Communists were in competition for working-class support, and for most of the time were hostile to each other. Second, though the traditional centre and right parties remained in general disparate and relatively unorganized, the influence between 1950 and 1954 of a strong and disciplined Gaullist party was lessened by the fact that like the Communist party it was opposed to the regime, and so could co-operate with the Communists to defeat governments but not to replace them. This helped to produce a more or less permanent state of deadlock that came to be called *immobilisme*.

Under the Fifth Republic, up to the end of the Gaullist decade and beyond, the co-operation between a dominant Gaullist party in the National Assembly and a Gaullist President in the Elysée, ensured stable governments. But there was still no coherent and permanent understanding between opposition parties, and hence no really effective parliamentary opposition. Two important changes in the relations between the Government parties occurred, however, after the end of the Gaullist decade. The Gaullist party, no longer under the influence of a charismatic leader, became itself less united, while, towards the end of the Giscardian septennate, the conservative Independent Republicans, who had been from the start partners in Gaullist governments, succeeded in transforming a number of centre and right groups into a single electoral organization supporting the President. The Union for French Democracy (UDF) as it was called, had, by 1978, increased its parliamentary representation to the point at which it threatened the position of the Gaullist party. On the opposition side, too, changes had occurred. In the early 1970s Socialists and Communists had improved their parliamentary position, following the drastic reduction in their numbers in the 1968 election held immediately after the left-wing strikes and demonstrations in May of that year. In 1972, they formed an electoral alliance on the basis of which they fought the election of 1973. They improved their position still more in the general election of 1978, and on the strength of those results, together with their candidate's challenge to the presidency of Giscard d'Estaing in 1974, were confidently looking forward to defeating him when he came up for re-election in 1981. Indeed, the policies and attitudes of the two left-wing parties were almost exclusively determined throughout most of the decade by their hopes of capturing the presidency in that year.

In any discussion of the French left, it is essential not to lose sight of three basic facts that are taken for granted in France, but that British observers sometimes tend to underestimate or overlook. The first is that, more than anything else, what characterizes the French left is the acknowledgment by its members (with only a few exceptions, such as the left-wing Radicals) of their common bond of acceptance of Marxist principles as the basis of their party attitudes. Though the word 'left', as used in France, has no equivalent in Britain (which uses the word in a quite different context) and is not easy to define, it has a universally recognizable quality in France which is essentially bound up with Marxist origins and loyalties, however much in reality Socialist brands of Marxism are remote from Communist conceptions. But both within and between the two parties the concept gives rise to unending dissensions. The result is that many of the left-wing controversies in France are neither understood nor appreciated in Great Britain, whose Labour movement – as the then secretary of the party told delegates to the International Socialist Conference in Copenhagen in 1950 – owes far more to Methodism than to Marxism.

The practical consequence of these differences between British and French Socialist parties is that, whereas there is little real interest among the majority of the rank and file on the British left in the subtleties and conflicting interpretations of Marxism, the subject has always been a source of passionate interest in France and also an important source of the left's divisions and party splits. And the second characteristic of the French left – its predilection for intellectual and ideological controversy and theorizing – is responsible for still further concentrating interest on theoretical and ideological principles, often to the virtual exclusion of concern with practical policies. Together, these two characteristics help to account for the greater attraction of Communism and the existence of a large Communist party, as well as for the permanent illusion of French Socialists that their common origins must somehow make it possible and desirable to reach an agreement between Socialists and Communists, a dream that has survived for decades without any convincing evidence to justify it.

The third characteristic which French Socialists and Communists share, and which intensifies the effects of the other two, is the almost permanent absence of the French left from power, and from the disciplines that the exercise of power inevitably impose. Whereas the British Labour party, unhampered by Communist rivalry and, until fairly recently, relatively immune from penetration by the ideological and often extreme-left fringe-groups that flourish in France, remained united enough to be able to exercise power five times covering a period of some twenty years between 1921 and 1981, French Socialists and Communists remained essentially opposition parties and so opposition-minded. Socialists only once formed a government (in 1936, supported by, but not joined by, the Communists, and surviving only about a year). And Socialists and Communists only once held office together (in the immediate post-war years, and in a tri-partite alliance with the predominantly Catholic Popular

Republican movement), an experience both brief and unhappy. Since 1947, the Communist party has had no representation in government, and since 1958 the Socialist party too has been consistently in opposition. As late as 1946, when a Labour government was in power in Great Britain, the Socialist leader, Léon Blum, was even advising members of the party not to concentrate too much of their attention on obtaining power.

The combination of these three factors has helped to maintain on the French left the permanent attraction of Socialist-Communist co-operation, at times going to the point of a search for unity between the two essentially rival parties.[1] The result has been a series of alternations between periods of Socialist-Communist *rapprochement* and periods of estrangement. The experiment of the Common Programme of 1972 was the most ambitious of the projects for common action, because, for the first time, there seemed to be a reasonable possibility of the two parties obtaining a parliamentary majority. It lasted longer and created more bitterness between them than any previous attempts. Whether the Socialist party learned any lasting lessons from it is doubtful. As the following summary indicates, there would seem little reason to believe that Socialist–Communist unity is any nearer than it has been over the past half-century. The permanent love-hate relationship remains intact.

Les frères ennemis and l'Union de la Gauche

The above brief background facts are, of course, familiar to all students of French politics. They have been summarized here only because they may help to explain to some British readers why French Socialists could persuade themselves that the attempt to form a union of the left, except for the most immediate practical electoral advantage, was not doomed to failure from the start. The basic facts regarding the attempt can be briefly summarized. After the 1965 agreement between Socialist and Communist parties to support a single candidate in the presidential election of that year, Socialists, Communists, left-wing Radicals and Mitterrand's *Convention des institutions républicaines* (a Socialist 'Club', not then part of the Socialist party) reached a preliminary agreement on further steps towards achieving united action. The Socialist Congress of 1969 agreed to give up any alliances with parties farther to the right, and to concentrate on efforts to achieve a union of the Socialist and Communist parties. But negotiations were long and difficult, and it was only on 27 June 1972 that they agreed on a Common Government Programme which was to be the platform on which the two parties fought the general election of the following year. In its introduction, the document was described as being not a Socialist programme but one providing for transition towards Socialism. The signatories described themselves as seeking to create an 'advanced democracy' (undefined) and the programme itself outlined the steps to be taken during the life of the following Parliament towards the ultimate goal of Socialism.

There were, from the beginning, ambiguities regarding the precise obligations accepted by the signatories, and suspicions on both sides regarding the likelihood of the provisions of the document ever being implemented. It was accompanied by the publication (independently) of two further programmes – the *Programme for a Democratic Government of Popular Union*, published some weeks earlier by the Communist party, and the *Government Programme of the Socialist Party*, published shortly after it. Though these two documents constituted the official programmes of the Communist and Socialist parties, no explanation was provided of the relation of these three documents to each other or to the Common Programme, on which both were to fight the election, or of the fact that there were discernible contradictions and incompatibilities between them. The three volumes – comprising some 700 pages in all – included detailed provisions for proposed legislation, presumably by a Socialist-Communist government. To quote one or two examples, the Socialist programme included acceptance of *l'autogestion* (worker participation or control) (pp. 69 ff.), decentralization (pp. 103 ff.) and the reorganization of Europe on the basis of common institutions (pp. 184 ff.), while the Communist document proclaimed that French foreign policy should be based on French independence and national sovereignty (p. 220), specifically rejected the idea of supranational institutions (p. 244), and remained silent on the subject of *autogestion*, an idea to which the Communist party was known to be adamantly opposed, and which, indeed, it did openly oppose both before and after the election campaign in 1973.

It is not possible to try to reconcile these differences on the ground that the common programme concerned only the next five years. For instance, a policy of European integration was incompatible with the retention of national sovereignty, and to 'seek the immediate dissolution of the North Atlantic and Warsaw alliances and the cessation of all nuclear production' was not only incompatible with fidelity to existing alliances but, unless it was intended to be no more than an empty phrase applicable to the Greek Kalends, also irreversible. The section of the programme dealing with *autogestion* (p. 111) clearly fudged the issue in what looks like a deliberate attempt to mislead.[2]

Leaving aside discrepancies or ambiguities, however, there were three specific points which aroused doubts and queries, indicating clearly that the attempt by the two parties to form a coalition government would not only encounter serious obstacles but would also be regarded by the signatories themselves with doubts and suspicions. To begin with, both insisted that only the numerical superiority of their own party would provide a guarantee that the programme would be carried out. In January 1973, for instance, the Communist party insisted, at a meeting held in Paris, and again the following month, that the Communist party *must* obtain more votes than the Socialists in the forthcoming general election's first ballot, as this would be the main guarantee that the programme would really be carried out. When asked whether the Communist party was the sole guarantor, the Communist party leader, Marchais, replied: 'On the basis of experience, yes.'[3] The Socialist party made a similar claim: 'The Common Programme of the Left', said Charles Hernu, Socialist defence spokesman, 'cannot be achieved unless Socialists and left-wing Radicals are the guarantors of democratic freedom.'[4]

If, after months of negotiation, the programme had created no more confidence than this on either side, it might be reasonable to conclude, on the basis of logic as well as experience, that the project might as well be abandoned.

The second point on which the Common Programme aroused anxiety, not only among Socialists but also in the government parties, was that it created doubts regarding the willingness of the Communist party to relinquish power once it had obtained it, even if the Government were to be defeated. This issue became one of the principal preoccupations during the 1973 election campaign. Both parties provided specific reassurances on the point, but there appeared to be significant differences between them. In his introduction to the Socialist programme, Mitterrand stated that:

> The Socialist party solemnly declares that its power depends wholly on universal suffrage and that it will form part of no coalition that does not undertake to abandon power if it is rejected by the electorate. (p. 24)

This assurance was repeated in the body of the programme (p. 33). The Communist party programme gave no specific or direct undertaking, merely referring in general terms, and in familiar Communist terminology, to 'the decisions of the people' and the satisfaction of 'the popular masses'. The Common Programme did, however, provide the following specific statement on the issue:

> If the majority parties were to lose the confidence of the country, they would resign and continue the struggle in opposition. But the democratic Government, whose existence implies the support of a majority of the people, will have as its main task the satisfaction of the working masses, and will, therefore, be strengthened by the confidence, ever more active, that they bring to it. (p. 149)

The second sentence – the 'petite phrase', as it was described in the press – attracted a great deal of comment. It appeared to be either meaningless or in contradiction with the previous one. Did it mean, merely, that such a situation was extremely unlikely, as the kind of government described would go from strength to strength? Or did it mean that, in case of a government defeat, the 'masses' would come to its aid – and if so, how? Was it a threat to take the battle into the streets? An ambiguous phrase in the Communist programme could have implied that the 'masses' would bring pressure to bear by demonstrations etc.? 'The intervention of the popular masses', it says, 'will certainly be necessary in order to translate these proposals into reality' (p. 35). And what, precisely, was to be understood by the initial 'But' in the second sentence? Did it mean that a government defeat need not be final because the struggle would continue outside Parliament? This last suggestion appeared to be the Communist position. In any case, Marchais gave a categorical affirmation of the Communist party's intention to 'remain resolutely on the side of legality and democracy and to neglect no effort to ensure respect for the democratic will as expressed through universal suffrage.' He spelled it out even more clearly in a broadcast a few days later, saying that, if the people were to refuse their confidence the party would not appeal to 'the masses' but would continue the fight in opposition.[5]

It is permissible to doubt whether much importance should ever have been attached to these assurances. It would certainly have been impossible to do so after the Communist leader, Marchais, had openly threatened during the presidential election campaign in 1981 to use strikes to ensure that Communist policies would be carried out, in the event of a Socialist victory.[6] But in 1973, in the atmosphere engendered on the left by the achievement of the Common Programme, some anxieties were evidently allayed by these Communist assurances. The importance attached to the issue in the 1973 election campaign nevertheless indicated that suspicions of Communist intentions were real, and not limited to government parties, although the Gaullists in particular exploited them.

The particular passage in the Common Programme that has been quoted was generally thought to have represented a compromise reached after a great deal of argument, in which the first sentence represented the Socialist and the second the Communist view. In which case, its obscurities did nothing to reassure those elements in the Socialist party that remained sceptical regarding the apparently sudden conversion of the Communist party to the principles of parliamentary democracy. Nor did another 'petite phrase' contributed by the leader of the Communist-dominated trade union confederation, the CGT, in which he appeared to be threatening trade union action to ensure, as he put it, that 'the will of the electorate' would be respected. The particular remark was described by a former Gaullist Minister as a threat 'to precipitate the country into economic chaos'.[7]

The third and by far the most important issue concerned the possible constitutional consequences of an electoral victory for the left. This was briefly mentioned in the last chapter in the context of its electoral repercussions. But the problem went deeper in that a situation was conceivable in which normal democratic parliamentary government could be rendered impossible, with all the dangers of political and constitutional instability that might ensue. In 1973 a victory of the left would have confronted a Gaullist President with a National Assembly dominated by political opponents. In 1974 a Socialist victory would have confronted a Socialist President with an Assembly in which there was a majority consisting of Giscardians and Gaullists not normally due for re-election until 1978. Both President Pompidou (in 1973) and President Giscard d'Estaing (in 1981) were questioned as to how they would deal with such a situation, and both had merely replied that they would behave with constitutional propriety.[8] In 1981 Mitterrand was to be actually faced with the problem, and promptly appealed for support in a general election.

What the Communists feared in 1973, however, was the effects on the Socialist-Communist alliance of such a situation. They feared that the Socialists might then be tempted to abandon the alliance and try to form a government including members of centre parties, and perhaps some Gaullists, leaving the Communists high and dry and with no option but to return to the 'ghetto' of isolation in opposition. However, in 1973 the government parties won the election, but the leaders of both government and opposition sides had, somewhat surprisingly, agreed to let the controversy drop some weeks before the election, declaring themselves satisfied with the President's assurances on the subject, no doubt, in reality, because it suited neither side to create the impression that a victory for the Common Programme might endanger the regime.

During the following seven years, Socialist-Communist relations went through two distinct phases. In the first, lasting up to 1976, they worsened after a brief lull in 1974 and 1975, caused in the first place by the presidential election following on Pompidou's sudden death, in which, as in 1965, the single candidate of the left was the Socialist leader, François Mitterrand; and in the second place by the Socialist party's preoccupation with its own internal reorganization, following the creation of a new party which absorbed several hitherto independent Clubs, among them the *Convention des Institutions républicaines* (CIR) led by Mitterrand, until he joined the new party as its leader in 1971. Throughout this period the two party leaders did not meet, and relations between Socialists and Communists became more and more strained.

One irritant was the widening gap between the concepts of Socialism being elaborated by the Socialist party and those of the Communist party. Nothing stimulates the French Socialist propensity for indulging in theoretical and utopian Socialist blueprints more than discussions on institutions. The first reaction of the party to reorganization was, therefore, to sit down and re-think its Socialist principles. In the course of discussions on prospects for a Socialist Europe, for the production of a comprehensive *Projet socialiste* and for a new Socialist manifesto (proposed by Guy Mollet), what emerged was that the centrepiece of these plans was to be the principle of *autogestion*. This was clearly going to be unacceptable to the Communist party, which, as has already been said, regarded it as a dangerous interference with the Communist interpretation of democratic management through 'democratic centralism', that is through agreements between state, firms and trade unions, applied and controlled from the top. Communists regarded *autogestion* as being liable – as they held the Yugoslav experiment to have shown – to create anarchy.

The issue of *autogestion* had been soft-pedalled during the election. Mitterrand was obliged by the support for this idea in his own party to appear at least sympathetic to it. His solution was to express a personal view as being in favour of it, but to qualify this by adding 'perhaps in five years' time'.[9] But the influx of new blood in the reconstituted party included a number of enthusiasts for *autogestion*, especially in the lively and aggressive minority movement CERES (*Centre d'Etudes, de Recherches et d'Education socialistes*), among former PSU (*Parti socialiste unifié*) members, including the influential Michel Rocard, and among members of the trade union movement CFDT (*Confédération française démocratique du Travail*). These groups, henceforth recognized minorities within the new party, were definitely more minority-minded and prone to indulge in theoretical or ideological speculation, irrespective of the need to think in terms of government responsibilities. Mitterrand did his best to restrain their *autogestionnaire* ardour in promoting what to a practical politician was no more than a 'gimmick', popular among the rank and file as promising the involvement of workers in what would have been in practice a Rousseauist form of direct democracy totally unadapted to the needs of modern technological systems, and conceivable, if at all, only in small units of production. Mitterrand had warned party members against committing themselves to the principle of *autogestion* before the party had reached a decision on it, and had even reproached the CERES movement (which was one of the most enthusiastic propagandists for it) for being 'real petits bourgeois trying to create an unreal Communisty party'.[10] Undeterred, CERES, having held a colloquium in 1974, produced a plan described as follows: '*Autogestion*, the Common Programme and the transition to Socialism – the reply to a new crisis of capitalism.'

And the final resolution of the 1975 Socialist Conference took a similar line, defining Socialism as being 'democratic and *autogestionnaire*.'

By this time, the *Union of the Left* was in the doldrums. Indeed, *Le Monde*'s correspondent, Thierry Pfister, described it at the beginning of 1975 as 'A framework within which each side is trying to get what it can for itself. Behind the façade of the Union of the Left, the rule is now: every man for himself.' And writing at the same time, Raymond Barrillon entitled an article on it simply 'The defunct Union of the Left'.[11]

From 1976, however, there seemed to be something of an attempt to revive it. The liaison committee of the two parties met twice in 1975, though the differences between the two parties were still unresolved. Socialists regarded the Communists as seeking to rely too exclusively on the class approach; Communists were accusing the Socialists of merely seeking – in the familiar Communist phraseology – to 'run capitalist concerns' (*gérer les affaires du capitalisme*); *autogestion* was still a sore point; and the Communist leader, Marchais, was adopting offensive and aggressive attitudes which did nothing to encourage reconciliation. He was by now suggesting that Communists and Socialists should fight the first ballot of the 1978 elections independently. Whether or not either side still believed in the so-called union, both continued to avoid meetings of the two party leaders, though the Common Programme, by now more than three years old, was clearly out of date on some points and in need of revision, or *actualisation* as it was called.

What must often have struck outside observers, and especially pragmatic British observers, as one of the characteristics and self-defeating attitudes of French reformers, especially on the left, is their tendency to produce plans, whether national or international, that totally ignore the known views of assumed or desired partners. The various plans for *autogestion* blandly ignored known Communist objections, just as the French advocates of a 'European Europe' in the 1960s had insisted on the need for Europe's independence from the United States, ignoring the known fact that every one of the proposed European partners was already committed to active membership of the Atlantic alliance and NATO. Germany, indeed, after the signature of the Franco-German treaty of 1963, creating what came to be called the Franco-German axis, went out of her way to remind

France of this fact, by including in the preamble to the law ratifying the agreement a specific reaffirmation of the German position. German policy, it said, was

> the maintenance and reinforcement of the Alliance of free peoples, and especially, a close association between Europe and the United States of America . . . common defence in the framework of the North Atlantic alliance and integration of the armed forces of the member states.

One possible explanation is that many French theoretical structures – and this applies especially to Socialist plans of various kinds – are not conceived of as being necessarily intended for implementation in the near future, but rather as so many intellectual frameworks within which to develop philosophical or political principles, seen as subjects for study or debate.

The Communist party was not idle during this period of apparent neglect of the idea of Union of the Left, but was making its own plans. Having put all its eggs into the Common Programme basket, it must now fall back on some alternative policy, if there was a real danger that the Socialist party might desert the alliance for some form of co-operation with non-left parties. This was all the more necessary in view of the fact that by now it was becoming more and more apparent that the Socialist party had derived more advantage from the alliance than had the Communists. The Communist solution was, therefore, one that had already been suggested in the early 1970s during a period when there had been a similar consciousness of Communist weakness, namely, to propose a *rapprochement* with the Gaullists, in the hope that their general agreement in the field of foreign policy would make it possible for them to vote for the Communists in the first ballot of the election, in order to oppose what was described as Atlanticism, or 'la petite Europe des trusts'. Such an appeal, said Marchais, was in accordance with the principles of the Champigny manifesto of 1968, when the electoral slogan of the Communist party had been :'Pour une démocratie avancée, pour une France socialiste'.

On the face of it, a convincing reason for this volte-face would seem hard to find. But the Communist party has surmounted more formidable logical obstacles. Marchais explained that, since the Common Programme was itself not Socialist but merely a transitional policy, and since there was, in any case, in the existing state of public opinion, no majority in the country for the Common Programme, he could at least try to obtain practical agreement between Communists and Gaullists on national defence objectives. This recall of a similar approach in 1968, described by the Communists as 'the historic compromise', did not receive a favourable reception, and the idea was in fact dropped.

From the beginning of 1976, however, prospects of Socialist-Communist agreement began to look a little brighter, though this turned out in reality to be merely a temporary phase of optimism. It lasted up to the final official break-up of the alliance in September 1977. The respite was made possible by a deliberate Communist attempt at fence-mending, directed towards those elements in the Socialist party anxious to be convinced of a Communist change of attitude, if any evidence could be found. At the twenty-second party Congress at the beginning of 1976, Marchais announced that the party had decided to abandon its doctrine of the necessity, during the period of transition to Socialism, of a period of dictatorship of the proletariat. The effects of this volte-face were sensational. At last, those who demanded democratic *bona fides* were presented with unchallengeable ones, on condition, of course, that it was possible to believe in the genuineness of the gesture. Second thoughts produced suggestions that so sudden a decision could perhaps be reversed with equal suddenness. But the reactions of the Soviet press certainly indicated that the Soviet Union at least believed in it and was appalled by it. The British reaction was incredulity. As one British correspondent put it, 'The rush to respectability of the French Communist party has left everyone a little breathless.'[12] French press reactions were mixed, some circles describing the decision as an obvious childish manoeuvre, others as a contribution to understanding between the Common Programme partners, and possibly an encouragement to some voters who might have voted Socialist now to feel it safe to vote Communist. It certainly produced one desired effect. During 1976, Communist party membership increased by between 50,000 and 100,000.

Though the revision of the Common Programme was now able to proceed, it did not prove possible for the would-be partners to come any nearer to agreement. There were differences on the projected figure for economic growth, on the number of additional nationalizations called for, on the accuracy of the Communist costing of these measures, the desirable level of the minimum wage level, wage differentials, and, of course, on defence. After four months of argument, the only subject on which the summit meeting of September 1977 could agree was its own agenda. The official break came on 22 September. The Common Programme went into cold storage, each side proclaiming that it still believed in it, but throwing the blame for the failure to reach agreement on the other. The main reason for this extraordinary situation was that, in view of the approaching general election, and the degree of support for a Socialist-Communist union among the rank and file of both parties, neither side wanted to take the responsibility for failure to achieve it and so both sides tried to salvage whatever party advantages they could.

Queries and problems

The obvious question was: Had the whole operation been a failure from the start, and did anything positive at all result from it? It certainly did nothing to contribute to the confidence of either party in the intentions of the other. On the Socialist side there were doubts regarding the possibility of Communist independence of Moscow and suspicions that Moscow had been using the French party for its own purposes. Whether these included or excluded readiness to see French Communists as members of a Socialist government was still an open question. But Moscow's readiness to accept Eurocommunism was not, for this was now under attack from Moscow. The Socialist leader had rejected Communist proposals for revision of the terms of the Common Programme, arguing that it would be time to think about a second programme when the first had been carried out. But the real truth was believed by the Socialist party to be that whatever had been the position at first, by now, neither Moscow nor the French Communist party wanted the agreement. Some Socialists too (in particular Michel Rocard) were arguing that the proposed Communist economic policies were not economically practicable. The Socialist National Convention in November 1977 approved of the following propositions: first, to ignore the Communist volte-face and continue to work for a union of the left; second, to oppose the Communist gesture towards the Gaullists – what the Communists described as the 'historic compromise' of temporary co-operation with a non-left party in the national interest; third, refusal to any commitment to include Communists in a Socialist government.

After the breakdown of negotiations, the Communist party simply went back to the comfortable position of conformity with Moscow. The proposal of *rapprochement* with the Gaullists – described as *l'Union du peuple de France* – had been abandoned in 1976, shortly after it had been made, as being incompatible with the Common Programme. It was now revived. The doctrine of democratic centralism was reaffirmed. At the twenty-third Communist Congress, in 1979, Marchais erased the memory of previous timid criticisms of Soviet policies by proclaiming that the balance sheet of the Socialist countries was 'globally positive'. And in 1980, the French Communist party approved of the Moscow policy regarding Afghanistan, now described as a victim of foreign imperialism. On this evidence, Jean Ellenstein, one of the most eloquent of the intellectual critics within the Communist party of its existing policies, concluded that the decisions of the previous Communist conference in 1976 could now be regarded as having been abandoned. Whatever the changes of course that the French Communist party was accusing the Socialist party of making, there was no doubt, he said, that the Communist party had 'veered to the East'.[13]

From then on, the Communist party's attitude towards the Socialists was one of systematic hostility and criticism.

As was to be expected, the Socialist party also resumed its familiar positions including work on the long talked-of Socialist Project. But the problem of who was to be the Socialist candidate in the forthcoming election now drove everything else into the background, a situation that continued until Mitterrand finally announced his decision to stand towards the end of 1980. Internal disunities persisted, increased by the rivalry between Mitterrand and Rocard as potential presidential candidates.

The conclusion must be that a decade's pursuit of a union of the left can only be regarded as wholly negative. But it would be unduly optimistic to conclude that the Socialist party had definitely abandoned it. In 1979, for instance, the Socialist party, in the face of the Communist barrage of attack, took the initiative of proposing the resumption of talks following a chilly and ambiguous remark of Marchais that he would 'unite with the devil in order to defeat the

Giscard-Barre policy'. But after a few weeks, the one meeting held broke up with no agreement. Marchais now rejected the whole idea of 'summit meetings' in favour of what he described as unity of action among the rank and file – which was obviously unachievable – and the Communist delegation turned down every suggestion made by the Socialists.

Can it be said that the Socialist party learned any useful lesson from these years of wasted energies and time? That, too, is doubtful. There were, however, some useful and pertinent comments made by qualified observers. Lionel Jospin, who had replaced Mitterrand as acting first secretary and was generally thought to be his probable permanent successor, gave an admirably complete and concise statement of the fundamental dilemma that must confront seekers after Socialist-Communist union:

> If the Socialist party is too weak, and especially electorally weak, then the left cannot obtain a majority in France. If the Socialist party is regarded by the Communist party as being too strong, then it will be opposed to the success of the union. Thus, victory is never possible.[14]

Yet he concluded by reaffirming party policy as still being that of a union of the left! Professor Maurice Duverger also pointed out the essential impossibility of a union of the left. It was plausible, he said, only on the assumption of unachievable changes in the Communist party. While it retained its monolithic structures, ideological intolerance and subservience to the Soviet Union, it was adapted for a Leninist dictatorship, not for the compromises demanded of democratic governments.[15] It was not clear, however, whether the 1977 breakdown had come on orders from Moscow or because the Communist party realized that the Socialists were deriving more benefit from the programme than they were. The editor of *Le Monde*, Jacques Fauvet, spelled out the situation even more clearly:

> The conclusion is that the left cannot govern, either with or without the Communists. Without Communist support, a government of the left cannot survive, unless it agrees to share government with the right. This is the contradiction that the Socialist party has been trying to escape from for ten years, by reorganizing and reforming its own institutions.

The Communist party, too, had its contradictions. As Jacques Fauvet pointed out:

> By repeating *ad nauseam* for three years that the Socialist party is 'veering to the right', it is hardly in a position to claim the right to hold office in a Socialist government.
> It should be added, moreover, that the question of Communist participation in a Socialist government will arise only after M. Mitterrand has succeeded in winning the election (an eventuality rendered less likely by Communist tactics) and after a dissolution of the National Assembly, which would probably follow.[16]

Critics of Socialist policy were faced, therefore, with the obvious question: what other possibilities were open to the party? There were surely only two. The party could go on hoping for a Communist change of heart, in spite of ten wasted years; this seemed what it would really prefer to do, mainly because it was and is essentially conservative and backward-looking and so is unable to change its fundamental attitudes, as successive Socialist programmes have made only too clear. The Communist party, too, however much it changes its policies, retains the familiar slogans and phrases that the rank and file are used to – invocations of the class struggle, claims to leadership of the working class, affirmations of the principle of democratic centralism and, since the 1960s, of the desire for 'an advanced democracy', whatever that may mean. Most important of all, a change of attitude remains impossible while the rank and file of both parties include numbers of party members who remain attached to the shared past before 1920, the dogmas of Marxism, the attachment to the concept of the reality of the 'left' and the common goal of something called Socialism (on which they certainly did not agree and probably never would) – a concept which, despite the Socialist passion for defining it and re-defining it, remained as elusive in theory as it was in practice, and more divisive than unifying.

At the Socialist Convention of January 1981, the new secretary-general, Lionel Jospin, reminded his audience that Socialist-Communist relations would not 'pass in a night from invective to smiles', a singularly inappropriate remark in the light of over three years of almost continuous Communist invective. The relevant question would have been whether the experiment of the Common Programme ought not to have demonstrated beyond any doubt the essential impossibility of a partnership between Socialists and Communists. For the party had seen the disappearance overnight of the desired Communist reassurances regarding Communist acceptance of democratic procedures, once the Communists had found that things were not going precisely as they had hoped. Instead of hoping to re-create what had proved to be an illusory union, ought not the party now to choose the second possible course of action – to decide that the smiles were meaningless and likely to remain so as long as one partner based its actions on doctrinaire, authoritarian principles laid down in practice in Moscow? In the 1940s, when the project of Socialist union was being mooted after the war, the Socialist leader, Léon Blum, had complained that 'the Communists combine French and Russian nationalism'. In the 1960s, the then Socialist leader had recognized that the Communist party belonged not so much to the left as to the east. In the 1980s, the reminders still appeared necessary. Léo Hamon, whose attempts at different periods to unite various parties either on the left or on the left of the Gaullist movement went back to that post-war period, concluded that the most useful lesson that the Socialist party could have, and ought to have, learned would have been to ask themselves 'how they would have managed to govern together, when they disagreed about everything'.[17] It appeared that the lesson still had to be learned.

The future of the left

The changed situation of the left from 1981 onwards means that speculations regarding its future cannot be divorced from the fortunes or misfortunes of a Socialist President. But a Socialist President – the first since 1947, when Presidents had no real power – is bound to be concerned by the effect on his own party of the unprecedented circumstances and incalculable consequences surrounding his assumption of office, especially as the party would be deprived of his effective leadership for the first time since it was formed in 1971. At least three specific problems were likely to have an important effect on the party's evolution. The first was its general attitude to the Communist party and to Socialist-Communist co-operation in particular. The question – after the Common Programme, what? – had been answered after a fashion by the production in 1979 and its amendment and acceptance in January 1980, of the long-awaited

Socialist Project. It did not appear to an outside observer to be significantly more down to earth than the Common Programme, on the up-dating of which Communists and Socialists had failed to reach agreement. It was noticeable, indeed, that during the election campaign Mitterrand himself had hardly mentioned it, preferring to rely on the Socialist Manifesto, agreed on at a special conference at the beginning of 1981, but drawn up by himself on the basis of the report of an *ad hoc* Commission. This document included a number of measures taken from the Socialist Project giving priority to policies concerned with economic growth, democratic liberties, the quality of life and foreign policy and announced a number of immediate steps to relieve unemployment and improve working conditions, but avoided any commitment to controversial left-wing ideological policies. It specifically rejected, for instance, 'all state monopolies', adding that 'nationalization is a means, not an end'.

The fact remained, however, that the Socialist Project was the party's official policy – its accepted alternative to the Common Programme. And although the President might intend to ignore it, there was no guarantee that the party would do the same or that there would not be a renewed effort, perhaps on the basis of the Project, to revive the idea of a union of the left. It had been largely drawn up by Jean-Pierre Chevènement, whose movement was anxious for Socialist-Communist *rapprochement*, and who might not be prepared to abandon it (especially if his ministerial appointment did not last). In some ways it might be acceptable to the Communist party as a basis for discussion. For instance, it emphasized the need for a class approach, for resistance to world capitalism, and reaffirmed the need for continued independence of Atlanticism. On the other hand, it still maintained Socialist attachment to *autogestion* (even if in somewhat muted terms). But, to the extent that it might appeal to Communists, it might well be a source of friction within the party, not all of whose members were sympathetic to Chevènement's approach.

For the moment, however, relations with the Communist party remained a matter of speculation. Its weakened position had created a new situation. Nothing indicated, however, that sooner or later, Socialist-Communist relations would not become again a divisive factor in the party. For the second problem, that of maintaining the cohesion of the Socialist party, was likely to play an important political role. Mitterrand's achievement in including four – or even five – distinct minority movements within the new Socialist party in 1971 had not meant that the voices of these minorities were silenced. Far from it. All the old divisions were clearly recognizable and their separate organizations persisted. There were the former supporters of Guy Mollet (now only a small group), members of Socialist Clubs, the left-wing CERES movement, the *autogestionnaire* movement headed by Michel Rocard, together with some members of the trade union confederation, the CFDT. Some of their differences from the Mitterrand-Mauroy-Defferre majority were marked. To weld them into a team providing support for presidential policies was not likely to prove an easy task. Nor was the existence of a large majority in the National Assembly likely to silence party critics. It might have the opposite effect, since there was now little risk of a government defeat in the Assembly.

The third problem, though wider, was not really separable from that of party unity. There were bound to be difficulties, even for a united party, in adapting nearly a quarter of a century's attitudes in opposition to the restraints and frustrations of government. Most members of the party were wholly inexperienced in government, the last regular government to include Socialist Ministers (two of them only!) having held office in 1958. Governments would, therefore, have their work cut out in dealing with the known difficulties of the existing economic situation, let alone those that were still to make themselves known. And over and above these preoccupations a Socialist President was bound to want to succeed in demonstrating to the satisfaction of party workers that even in the difficult conditions of the 1980s, the Government was achieving the first steps along the road to an orderly transition to the long hoped-for goal of Socialism.

4 Problems of the right

If the main problem of the left has been the extent to which its policies and attitudes remain bound up with its past, that of the right has been that it has too little past, or in the case of the Gaullists only a recent past that played too large a part in its current thinking, since it was born in a uniquely dramatic situation under the leadership of a unique personality. Throughout the Fifth Republic, the two main components of the government majority in the National Assembly remained the Gaullist party under the five different names that it gave itself between 1958 and 1980, and its junior partner, known in 1958 as the Independent Republicans, whose history goes back to the Fourth Republic and of which Giscard d'Estaing was an acknowledged leader until he became President of the Republic.

General de Gaulle founded the *Rassemblement du Peuple français* (RPF) in 1947, and from 1951 it was to all intents and purposes a political party, being represented in the National Assembly until 1953 by some hundred or more Deputies, reduced to a rump of seventy in 1954 and about twenty in 1956 by the disbandment of the Gaullist movement and General de Gaulle's withdrawal of his association with it. In the first Parliament of the Fifth Republic, under the title of *Union pour la nouvelle République (UNR)* the Gaullists obtained 199 seats and remained for the following twenty-three years the dominating party, unchallenged until 1978.

Its existing constitution dates only from 1976, following the re-organization of the party between 1974 and 1976 under the presidency of Jacques Chirac. There had always been elements in it which resisted the evolution into a party, hoping to retain its original appeal as a *rassemblement* with a national leader, but in the post-Gaullist era charismatic leaders were in short supply and the party needed the conventional paraphernalia of committees and executives in order to compete effectively in party politics and electioneering. In the earlier years of the 1970s, Gaullists found difficulty in adapting to political life without de Gaulle. They feared that perhaps behind the familiar phrases and slogans there might now be merely a vacuum and that they had lost their sense of purpose.

The other component of the government majority had been until the end of the 1960s very much the junior supporting party. It consisted of the relatively small orthodox conservative Independent Republican party and from 1969 onwards representatives of the Centrist groups in the National Assembly. In 1978, however, together with two other small parties, one of which was the Radical party, they formed an electoral coalition, the Union for French Democracy (UDF) with the purpose of providing a party supporting President Giscard d'Estaing and hoping to challenge the hitherto dominant Gaullist party. These two formed an uneasy and divided partnership held together mainly by the danger that if they did not hang together both risked defeat by the left, whose accession to power seemed increasingly within the bounds of possibility from 1965 onwards.

Though described by the left as representing the right, the government partnership describes itself as *la majorité*. The difference between the two concepts is seen by J. R. Frears as being essentially that

> The *Majorité* is more than a coalition but less than a party. It is a term that embraces all parties and groups that give disciplined electoral and parliamentary support to the President of the Republic and the Government appointed by him. The presidential element is of great importance. It is the components of his support that define the *Majorité*, but the term can only be used when the President has the support of the parliamentary majority in the National Assembly.[1]

The main problem of the *majorité* during the Giscardian septennate was, therefore, to prevent the permanent and increasing differences between Gaullists, who formed the largest party in the National Assembly, and 'Giscardians', as their partners began to call themselves, from developing into a crisis involving the danger of a government defeat. Their relations with each other were very different from those of the two main opposition parties, Socialists and Communists, and, perhaps mainly because they did not form part of familiar French political history, were on the whole less publicized. Neither party was an ideological party (unless Gaullist principles can be described as an ideology, which many Gaullists would deny). Both accepted the existing system of presidential, or semi-presidential, government and had no desire to introduce constitutional reforms. Neither wished to see any wholesale reform in the existing organization of French society.

What, then, did they quarrel about? There were differences on policies. For instance, the more conservative Giscardians (and also Gaullists on the right wing of the party) had little sympathy in general with Gaullist more progressive ideas, such as 'participation', or even for the idea of contractual collective bargaining (*la concertation*) associated with the policies of Chaban-Delmas when he was Prime Minister under the presidency of Pompidou. Indeed the concept of a 'new society' associated with Chaban-Delmas, and of which this policy was a part, was suspect to a number of his own party as well as to the Giscardians. The Gaullists, for their part, were suspicious of Giscard d'Estaing's often-expressed desire for a widening of the Government's basis to include Centrist elements, especially members of parties regarded as either supporters of an integrated Europe or suspected of sympathy with Atlanticism. Giscard d'Estaing himself was, indeed, not regarded as being wholly reliable as a supporter of the Gaullist doctrine of national independence from both the United States and NATO, and of hostility to all moves towards greater integration in Europe.

Gaullists and Giscardians 1974–1976

The differences between them concerned permanent attitudes rather than specific policies and were clearly visible at the time of the elections to the European Assembly in 1979. They were in the main expressions of political rivalry, both organizations having as their dominant aim to capture the presidency. There were, however, specific irritants and preoccupations at different periods. The Gaullist-Giscardian duel went through three successive phases between 1974 and 1981 during which the hostility between the two leaders, the President and the Gaullist leader, Chirac, became steadily more pronounced. The two men were, in fact, both temperamentally and politically incompatible. The former Prime Minister's vigorous and electoralist approach made him increasingly intolerant of the elegant and discreet reformism of the President. He resented what he regarded as presidential slowness and also unexpected innovations. Above all, he disliked the presidential style. And so, although the relationship began well, and the appointment of a Gaullist Prime Minister helped to reconcile the Gaullists to a non-Gaullist President, by 1976 irritation and incomprehension had produced conflict, the resignation of Chirac and the publicization of the differences between Prime Minister and President.

The Gaullist party at this period was going through a difficult phase in adapting itself to the loss of both General de Gaulle and Pompidou. The latter, though not wholly acceptable to what might be termed the more 'fundamentalist' Gaullists, had provided a familiar presence at the head of affairs following a six-year premiership, and without him the party suffered what was described by some commentators as 'a veritable crisis of identity'. When de Gaulle died, Pompidou had described France as being 'widowed'. When he himself was no longer there the party felt doubly bereft.

To begin with, it was leaderless. Neither de Gaulle nor Pompidou had occupied the position of formal leader of the party, though they were indubitably its effective and accepted leaders. And when Chaban-Delmas had suggested, when he was Prime Minister, that the party should elect a leader, the President had been opposed to such a step on the ground that it was unnecessary while he was there. But in 1974 there was no obvious heir. Chaban-Delmas himself was too far to the left of the party for some and was also unacceptable for other reasons, and, though there were some half-dozen Gaullist leaders of the first vintage – Olivier Guichard, Gilbert Grandval, for instance, together with Michel Debré, who undoubtedly had the required standing – none was wholly acceptable. Debré himself was for many a too whole-hearted disciple – almost a Gaullist prophet – and a man of the past rather than of the future, not sufficiently in touch with the younger generation of would-be Gaullist leaders.

Problems of the right 51

The problem of the organization of the party in order to equip it for efficient political and electoral propaganda was also urgent. There had grown up alongside it an increasing number of Gaullist fringe groups – 'Clubs', *groupes d'etudes*, or semi-independent parties, some claiming to be farther to the left, some associated more with personalities than with any clearly defined differences of principle, some forming separate youth movements – and so on. In 1973, nine of these organizations decided to publish a study of the fundamental principles of Gaullism.[2] This problem was no doubt a symptom of the sense of loss of purpose or identity that characterized the Gaullist movement at this time. Unfortunately, however, they did not throw much light on the subject and some of the fringe movements refused to be associated with them. A brief statement issued by them to the press consisted mainly of quotations from de Gaulle's speeches or writings and paraphrases of some of his remarks.

One question being discussed was whether or not the party had an ideology, or a doctrine. Pompidou had displeased some of the old guard by saying that Gaullism was 'not a doctrine but an attitude'.[3] Gaullist objectors had replied that de Gaulle himself believed that Gaullism did have a doctrine. The party's constitutional expert, Marcel Prélot, even described 'Pompidolisme' as 'a heresy'.

This question was not satisfactorily answered, but one question did appear to have been settled by 1976. At least the party was conscious of having if not a dogma then recognizable and accepted principles. Though the policy themes outlined in 1975 were very vague and general, they did say something. The main themes were participation, the decentralization of industry, the reduction of inequalities, reforms of the condition of the workers, and improvements in public transport.

Perhaps the best description of Gaullism was that it was distinguishable by three essential principles: fidelity to the institutions of the Fifth Republic; a belief, at least in theory, in the need to transform social conditions, mainly by means of the policy of participation; and the doctrine of 'national independence' in the field of foreign policy. The belief in participation was not widely shared, even in the party. Neither in France nor in Great Britain has the bulk of the population ever shown much interest in the idea of participation, either in profits or in management, in spite of the attraction that such theories have had for political reformers, especially on the left. In France, both in employers' organizations and trade unions, there was a good deal of positive opposition to it, in the latter case mainly on the ground that if applied these principles would blur the divisions on which, in their view, the class war depended. Still, the idea did differentiate Giscardians and Gaullists, for the former were much closer to the employers' and trade union views. Some right-wing elements in the Gaullist party were also somewhat wary of it. Since the idea of national independence was subscribed to by all parties in France from left to right it could hardly be held to be only a Gaullist principle. But it was first formulated by General de Gaulle and the strength of its attraction remained apparently undiminished after his death. It was also throughout the Giscardian septennate one of the most persistent subjects of disagreement between Giscardians and Gaullists, not in principle, but in the details of its practical application and in the permanent Gaullist suspicion that the Giscardians were lukewarm about it and might succumb to the temptations of Atlanticism.

From 1976 onwards the period of heartsearching seemed to be over, perhaps mainly because, thanks to the skill and persistence of Jacques Chirac, the Gaullist organization was demonstrably that of a party. The task had not been carried out without difficulty, for there were three main tendencies discernible regarding this question. The older generation of Gaullist leaders, and especially the most formidable exponent of the pure Gaullist word, Michel Debré, remained opposed to the transformation of Gaullism into a conventional political party. But a brief consultation of the figures had made it clear that without a more formal structure the existing small membership, mainly concentrated in predominantly conservative and Catholic regions and with its age composition mainly in the forties to sixties, would not be capable of maintaining Gaullist domination of the National Assembly, and that was essential for the implementation of presidential policies and for the popularization of specifically Gaullist objectives. The attitude of the first generation Gaullists was summed up in the comment made by Gilbert Grandval, leader of a fringe Gaullist group: 'a *rassemblement* reduced to the role of a party, a Prime Minister who is a politician. What could be less Gaullist?'[4]

Chirac, whose aim was power, could not try to make the Gaullist party a citadel of power without risking an actual decline in its political influence. And there were plenty of Gaullists who agreed with him. Chirac's generation believed – as Pompidou had believed – that the party must have an efficient and modern machine geared to vote winning and propaganda. There were also a number of run-of-the-mill Gaullist politicians whose main interest was not Gaullist ideas but how to retain their seats in the next elections, and especially how to defeat a rival Giscardian candidate. These two categories were not always easy in practice to distinguish because personal factors complicated the situation. Some Gaullists did and others did not want Chirac to be the party leader. Some preferred Chaban-Delmas. Others were politically almost indistinguishable from Giscardians outside the field of foreign policy and were prepared to go some way with Giscard d'Estaing. This was, at first, Chirac's own attitude, for he and the forty-three Gaullists he carried with him were certainly instrumental in securing the defeat of the Gaullist candidate, Chaban-Delmas, in the first ballot in 1974 and so ensuring the election of Giscard d'Estaing to the presidency.

Some Gaullists who favoured the view that Gaullism must be a political party certainly did not want Chirac to be its leader and did not necessarily want the organization to be along 'Chiraquian' lines – personalities such as Robert Boulin, Lucien Neuwirth, and the leader of the parliamentary Gaullist group were all in different ways doubtful regarding Chirac, or even hostile to him. He was, however, supported during these years by Alexandre Sanguinetti, who represented the tendency that believed conditional support for Giscard d'Estaing to be possible – whose attitude was in his own words one of 'oui-si', that is, support of Giscard d'Estaing's presidential options until such time as it could be seen whether or not he really intended to put them into practice.

This degree of confusion in the party meant that there was not unanimous approval of Chirac's appointment in 1974 as secretary-general. As Prime Minister he was entrusted by the President with the specific task of party reorganization, but was obliged to resign this task owing to hostility to his holding the two posts of Prime Minister and secretary-general of the Gaullist party. The increasing friction between himself and the President became evident, however, during the following two years, and when he resigned in 1976 as Prime Minister, he was forthwith elected president of the Gaullist party. He then completed the reorganization, including a change of name from

UDR (*Union des démocrates pour la République*) to RPR (*Rassemblement pour la République* – the title it held throughout the septennate), secured his re-election to Parliament as Deputy for his constituency in the Corrèze, and rapidly established himself as leader of a party which was no longer what Jean Charlot had described it as in 1970:

> a curious party . . . born with political power in its cradle; it won an electoral triumph before it had the time to organize . . . a ministerial team, then a central committee for the selection of candidates in parliamentary elections, thirdly the largest parliamentary group in the National Assembly and only lastly a party.[5]

Giscard d'Estaing was thought to have entrusted the task of party reorganization to Chirac in the hope that he would 'Giscardize' it. What he did was to make it a 'Chiraquian' party.

Gaullists and Giscardians 1976–8: the President's men

During the second phase of the Gaullist-Giscardian duel, during which Chirac's main purpose appeared to some observers to be to make himself the President's public enemy number one, the Giscardians began to realize that they were not efficiently organized to compete with the more disciplined and powerful Gaullist party. The two years leading up to the 1978 general election were naturally dominated by electoral preoccupations, since both government partners had as their main aim to dominate the majority. The Gaullists had the numbers but the President had the power and attraction of presidential office, though his supporters had been from the beginning of the regime the junior partner. The Independent Republicans had never numbered more than 50–60 Deputies, and the supporting centre groups were independent parties anxious to maintain their own identities and so not necessarily to be counted on as permanent presidential allies. The attempt during these years to weld these heterogeneous elements into a reliable electoral alliance as a basis for a hoped-for federation was, therefore, bound to encounter problems and difficulties. There could be no question of a merger. It was clearly going to be difficult enough to persuade them to form a loose electoral association, as indeed the negotiations of 1977 and 1978 demonstrated.

The President himself had always been known to favour a widening of the basis of government in order to include Centrists, and perhaps even left-centre or left members. As he stated in 1971, France wanted to be governed from the centre. Chaban-Delmas had included in his 1968 government four Centrist members, as evidence of his belief in 'a new society' and his successor in 1972 had done the same. Giscard d'Estaing, in his first government reversed the proportions, reducing Gaullist Ministers to four and increasing the representation of Independent Republicans, Centrists and non-party presidential supporters to eleven. The fact remained, however, that the centre groups remained independent parties, and that a profusion of candidates in the election could cost the Giscardians a number of seats. From 1977 onwards, therefore, a veritable team of Giscardians close to the President set out deliberately to try to create a single electoral entity in support of the President. The task proved long, complex and difficult and setbacks were numerous.

The majority was, at this point, facing three major problems. The first was that of the increasing friction between the two partners, both on policies and on tactics. Chirac's main interest was centred on the need to prepare for the 1978 election, which he feared might be won by the left unless greater efforts were made. The President appeared to him to be primarily interested in his policies connected with 'advanced liberalism', and in particular the introduction of a capital gains tax, highly unpopular with many Gaullists and with a number of Giscardians. It was finally voted in June 1976, but had created much ill feeling. There had also been friction regarding the liberalization of the rules governing abortion and contraception. There were known differences in defence policy (discussed in a later chapter), where the President's objectives appeared to Chirac vague, whereas his own were clear enough. On electoral tactics, however, there were problems that required immediate action, for instance the nature of the electoral agreements between the two partners in the first ballot and who was to lead the campaign, Chirac or the Prime Minister – who did not seem to covet the task. And while attempts were made to work out a code of conduct, the proposed presidential electoral alliance was hanging fire and no common programme came in sight until September 1977, when a vague manifesto was issued on essential principles.

Though both parties declared that the majority was united, they proceeded to demonstrate that they were not. Chirac made a party appeal for a nation-wide tour. Raymond Barre gave a television interview outlining the Government's objectives but failed to make clear the relation of these to the manifesto, while Jean-Pierre Fourcade, the leader of the influential Giscardian Club, *Perspectives et réalités*, presented four main themes of his own, described as objectives or common proposals. They were: to respond adequately to the daily needs of the French people; to create a society in which there was more justice and solidarity; to increase responsibility at all levels; and to make France a respected and outward looking power. The impact of this was, not surprisingly, nil. The press at that time was far more interested in the breakdown of the left's Common Programme.

At this stage it looked as if all parties would insist on fighting the election on the basis of their own programmes, thus reducing the desired federation of the Giscardians to an organization for sharing out seats between representatives of the various groups. Chirac was still in favour of independent voting in the first ballot, a course which would have benefited the Gaullists with their greater cohesion and greater numbers of candidates.

The second problem was the worsening of the personal relationship between the President and Chirac as exemplified by the incident in May 1977 when Chirac, in a gesture that looked like deliberate provocation, insisted on opposing the candidate favoured by the President for the recently created post of Mayor of Paris. He succeeded in getting himself elected and in using that vantage point to publicize at least one serious disagreement with the Government. Since the election and this dispute filled the columns of the press for weeks, the general impression of disunity within the majority's ranks was further increased, as it was by the prospect – much discussed – of Chirac's candidature for the presidency in 1981. There appeared to be a growing conviction among observers that, in the words of one of them, 'The Giscardian and Gaullist camps are henceforth virtually irreconcilable,'[6] a view not contradicted by Chirac's comment on the state of affairs: 'There is no longer a Fifth Republic. Our institutions are misused. They are Gaullist institutions in the hands of Vichyites.'[7]

And in a speech to some thousand or more representatives of the RPR in Paris, given in September 1980 on his return to political activity after a virtual silence since the European election the previous June, he delivered the following condemnation of the existing political situation: It was, he said,

> a situation of carefully encouraged anaesthesia. In July Cambodians are massacred and nobody cares; prices go up by 1 per cent in July and nobody cares; the Russians invade Afghanistan and nobody cares; there are a million and a half unemployed and nobody cares. We continue to snore and nobody wakes us up. But the risk is of an awakening that is too late to avoid misfortune, tragedy and catastrophe.[8]

This indictment would have carried more weight if Chirac's party had not been the dominant partner in the Government presumably responsible for this situation, a government, moreover, that had deliberately been spared by the Gaullist-dominated majority in the National Assembly from the expression of criticism by a vote of censure. As Raymond Barrillon asked pertinently: when did Chirac condemn as dangerous and intolerable a regime that he had supported over the past seven years, and now seemed to be regarding as the responsibility of one man, the rest being regarded as submissive, irresponsible or unaware subjects?[9]

The third problem, of course, was that of the future of the proposed Giscardian *rassemblement*. Its immediate future remained in doubt up to the weeks preceding the election, and even then it is perhaps not being too cynical to suggest that the final birth of what was called the Union for French Democracy (UDF) owed more to fears of the electoral consequences of the recent regulation requiring candidates to poll 12 per cent of the vote in the first ballot to be eligible to stand in the second than to differences of policy. For a proliferation of competing Giscardist, Centrist and Radical candidates would have been annihilated.

Finally formed in February 1978, the UDF consisted of three main elements: Conservatives, represented by the *Parti républicain* of which Giscard d'Estaing has been the leader, and the associated group of Clubs, *Perspectives et réalités*, founded by him and whose President was a conservative Senator, Jean-Pierre Fourcade; Centrists, made up of the *Centre des Démocrates sociaux*, itself created by the fusion of two Centrist movements, and whose leader was Jean Lecanuet, who also became President of the UDF; and the Radical party led by Jean-Jacques Servan-Schreiber. Three small political organizations were also included: the *Mouvement démocrate socialiste de France*, led by a former right-wing Socialist, Max Lejeune; and two small survivors of the Fourth Republic, the conservative *Centre national des Indépendants et Paysans* and the almost defunct right-wing radical movement, the *Centre républicain*. How far the new formation would survive once the immediate electoral challenge was past was still an open question and remained up to and beyond the presidential election a matter for speculation and anxiety, for its *raison d'être* had been support of the President and his defeat therefore created a new situation.

For the time being, however, the efforts of the negotiators met with a success beyond their expectations. The figures of the 1978 election spoke for themselves. When Parliament met in April 1978, Gaullists and associates numbered 154, while Deputies elected under the UDF banner numbered 123. The voting figures were even more eloquent. Out of a total registered electorate of 35,204,102, over 82 per cent had voted. Just under six million had voted for the UDF and six million for the Gaullists. A few hundreds of thousands had voted for candidates describing themselves merely as supporters of the President. This result was acclaimed by those who had struggled to produce the new federation with an optimism that later events did not justify.

> The emergence in French political life of the new Giscardians threatens twenty years of Gaullist domination of the governmental majority, and possibly opens the way to further even more profound changes after 1981. With the UDF, nothing in the political debate of the Fifth Republic will ever be the same again.[10]

Not all observers shared this optimism after the presidential election.

Gaullists and Giscardians 1978–81

The third phase in the relationship between Gaullists and Giscardians was wholly concerned with electoralism and characterized by still greater political acerbity between the two rival leaders, who now became rival presidential candidates. Electoral prospects were exceedingly difficult to forecast, largely owing to the complicated tactics of the Communist party and to the uncertainties regarding the effects of the proliferation of Gaullist candidates. Since three of the four were bound to be defeated in the first ballot, and probably all four, their recommendations to their supporters in relation to the second ballot would be important, and might even prove vital. Nobody at that stage seemed seriously to be considering the possibility that the President would actually be defeated. But it would certainly embarrass the President if Chirac were to succeed in defeating Mitterrand in the first ballot, thus creating a situation in which the second would be a public Giscard-Chirac duel. But assuming, as most people did, that the second ballot would be between Giscard d'Estaing and Mitterrand, it was vital that the former should be able to count on the votes of Chirac's supporters, and it was known that he was personally unpopular with some elements in the Gaullist party who might, perhaps, choose Mitterrand in preference to him.

Much, therefore, depended on the personalities and the performance of the two men. In reality, when the expected duel took place, it was in an atmosphere very different from what it had been in 1974. Both candidates were in some respects vulnerable. The President was an unknown factor in 1974. In 1981 he was faced with the problem of explaining why he had failed to come up to the expectations of electors since then. Mitterrand was now seven years older, fighting his third, and obviously last, presidential contest, and with the incalculable burden of his association with the Communist party over most of that period. Both must have been well aware of the fact that the French electorate – especially on the left – appeared to exhibit a fundamental stability in spite of the vicissitudes of party quarrels. And both must have been well aware that whichever of them won was going to be faced with difficult and perhaps dangerous problems. The events of the septennate had also created problems regarding the future of government parties themselves.

1981 – the problem of the UDF

As far as parties on the government side were concerned, the most immediate and obvious problem after the election was whether the UDF had a future at all. It was still no more than an electoral federation whose only real *raison d'être* had been support for the President. Its long and painful gestation, the reservations exhibited by some of the Centre elements, which had been no more than papered over, did not encourage optimism. The Republican party's orthodox conservatives, if they had some sympathy for the remnants of Atlanticism among the centre groups, did not necessarily share Jean Lecanuet's party's heritage of progressive Catholicism, and even less the Radical views of Jean-Jacques Servan-Schreiber, whose inclusion in the UDF could perhaps be regarded as a gesture towards Giscard d'Estaing's professed desire for government from the centre and for 'advanced liberalism'.

The movement's essential heterogeneity remained, indeed, not only its chief obstacle as a would-be party but its outstanding difference from the other three main parties. Everybody knew what a Gaullist party, a Socialist party, a Communist party stood for, but what was the UDF other than a Giscardian party? And what was a Giscardian party to be when Giscard d'Estaing was no longer President?

The following acute, evocative and disturbing portrait of the UDF, given by Alain Duhamel in his *République giscardienne*, makes the scale of the problem clear. It was, he said,

> a strange agglomeration of traditional moderates and former Socialists, of determined reformers and hoary conservatives, of landowners from Mayenne and Deux-Sèvres, of Alsatian office workers and Southern lawyers, teachers from Picardy, industrialists from Burgundy, Paris civil servants and mothers from middle-class quarters of Paris. ... a coalition of practising Catholics, convinced freemasons, MRP supporters and traditional Radical committees, of conservative '*notables*' and up-and-coming businessmen, a new kind of alliance between temple and chapel, landed proprietors and United States-trained engineers, those whose hearts are on the centre-left and their wallets on the centre-right, a strange assortment and a quite new mixture, a kind of Spanish Inn where everyone brings his own food and cutlery, yet gets used to eating at his usual table.[11]

The instinctive and traditional party dislike of discipline among those members who claimed to be Centrists or liberals militated against any organization as binding as a confederation, let alone a federation. If the separate histories of the different member parties are anything to go on, then the absence of a specific and immediate electoral challenge would be more likely to produce disintegration than to encourage moves towards integration.

The first reaction of some UDF members to the announcement in May 1981 of the dissolution of Parliament and an immediate general election, far from revealing the determination to keep the different elements together, seemed more like a move to desert a sinking ship, for Lecanuet, its President, lost no time in nailing its electoral flag to the Chiraquian mast. And when the campaign officially opened on 1 June, there was still none of the apparent convergence between different elements that had appeared to characterize the party when it fought the 1978 election as the President's party. This was perhaps not surprising, since the former President was absent from the scene and the news, and his future intentions unknown. By contrast, the Gaullist leader Chirac, encouraged by his creditable electoral achievement in the presidential election, was clearly determined to take advantage of the obvious disarray of the UDF to try to restore the Gaullist party to its former position of dominant party in the National Assembly. And his energy and organizing ability, together with the strength and relative coherence of the Gaullist party, made him a formidable electoral opponent.

The much commented on personal hostility between the two previous leaders, while potentially serious on the hypothesis that they would have to govern together in the event of a right-wing electoral victory, had been more dangerous when one was President and the other his resentful former Prime Minister. But in the event of Giscard d'Estaing's return to politics and to leadership of a political party, how serious would this prove to be when he was no longer President, especially if, as was by then generally expected, both parties would be in opposition? In one sense, the personal hostility had been useful to the UDF because it had helped to focus on the leadership of the President its heterogeneous elements, bound together in the main only by the common acceptance of 'Giscardism' and a common dislike for Gaullism. But what was 'Giscardism', either without Giscard d'Estaing or with him, when it could no longer be identified with his appeal as President?

Was Giscardism necessary? Does it exist?

If the survival of the UDF was problematical without the leadership of the President, whose instrument it had been created to be, was the survival of Giscard d'Estaing as a front-rank political leader conceivable without something hitherto called Giscardism? In the new circumstances, if the UDF was to survive and to maintain the support that it had visibly attracted in the country it needed more to hold it together than a man who had been President, and might be President again. Not that these considerations were unimportant. Giscard d'Estaing was a young man. He could afford to wait. The fortunes of parties change, and, if the Socialist President failed to satisfy the expectations of his supporters, there could be a swing back again to support for the former government parties. But would it be to the Gaullists or to the UDF, if it survived?

The answer to this question lies in the capacity of the UDF, or some organization based on the parties forming it, to find something as well as someone to hold it together, whether it is called Giscardism or something else. It is not so much the nature of the ideas making up what holds a party together that matters as its capacity to convey the feeling of 'belonging', of identity. Radicalism has always been a recognizable concept and Radicals have had no difficulty in identifying themselves with Radical organizations without any specific body of accepted principles. The position of Edgar Faure is an example of this approach. When he claimed to be still a Radical, while being in fact a Gaullist Deputy, everybody knew what he meant even if they disagreed with the approach. A man of the left is recognizable and prepared to continue to be so without the need for a clear idea of what being left implies. Gaullists do not always agree on what Gaullism is, but they know when they are Gaullists. The problem of the UDF, if it wants to be a party, is that it needs a focus that gives it a sense of identity. Once the formative period is past and it has become a party, it can continue to survive as such provided the label is satisfactory to the members. This was the point grasped by Chirac about Gaullism, and that 'historic' Gaullists failed to understand. A *rassemblement* was not enough. Gaullism needed to have (or to have had) a leader, and to have an organized political machine whose members regarded themselves as Gaullists, and that is what Chirac's re-organization of the party in 1976 provided.

The vital questions were: does Giscard d'Estaing want to create a Giscardian party and, if so, will he be an acceptable leader? Will his concepts of Giscardism be acceptable? In his book, already referred to, Alain Duhamel claims that there is such a thing as 'Giscardism', that Giscard d'Estaing does have an ideology, and that he has formulated it in his book *Démocratie française*. It adds up, he says, to a spirit of modernism or neo-liberalism, a notion of France as being made up of the concepts of pluralism, unity and personal responsibility. To ask 'Is that enough?' or to object to the concept of 'une société libérale avancée' as, in the words of a Gaullist critic, 'an idea to which it is very difficult to attach any real meaning'[12] are both essentially irrelevant objections. The only thing that matters is whether it satisfies would-be Giscardians. Some French people did not find General de Gaulle's concepts, described by him as 'une certaine idée de la France', either credible or particularly meaningful, but it satisfied Gaullists, as did his developments of it, such as 'European Europe' and 'national independence'. If Giscard d'Estaing's 'advanced liberalism' can give the UDF a comparable sense of *raison d'être* and collective identity with a comparable rallying power, then it could become a party.

So far, it had not been made clear that he wanted to lead that party. He himself had categorically denied that he did. 'I should like', he said in the course of a speech in May 1979, 'the French debate to become more depersonalized, more of a real debate on choices and ideas.' Why, he asked his audience, do you want to have Giscardians?[13] A few weeks earlier, he had expressed similar views in a television programme. 'I am not interested', he said, 'in what my future career is to be, and I do not support the personalization of power. I do not ask anybody to be Giscardian.'[14] He may not have regarded himself as a Giscardian, just as General de Gaulle did not call himself a Gaullist, but those who supported him clearly regarded themselves as Giscardians. The position of a President is unique, however, and General de Gaulle always endeavoured to hold himself aloof from the party that supported him – not always successfully, any more than were President Giscard d'Estaing's efforts.

If, when in opposition, he changed his mind, would he be an acceptable leader? That is a question very difficult to try to answer. What is clear from a number of comments by French commentators and critics, from the evidence of opinion polls and from the electoral statistics of the presidential election, is that he made enemies as well as attracted supporters. It would seem that if he wished to remain a possible future presidential candidate, he would do well to take note of at least some comments indicating that in spite of his generally recognized qualities he had sometimes been felt to lack something that a national leader needs. It probably needs a war or a national crisis to evoke the kind of response that a de Gaulle or a Churchill evoked. But a political leader must, to be successful, create some sense of human contact. It is doubts on this score that more than anything else appear to disturb his compatriots, as the following comments on some of his television performances and press conferences indicate. 'One asks oneself,' wrote a commentator, 'whether, behind all the analyses divided into three parts, the learned résumés, the total familiarity with the dossiers and the clarity of the exposé, there is any conviction, any human approach, any solidarity.'[15] Another critic described his manner as 'incurably remote, at times out of touch with day-to-day realities'.[16] His talks were also described as 'a pedagogic exercise',[17] and his style criticized as being one of 'reassuring moderation, dominated by coquetry, a certain remoteness and good taste'.[18]

In the recent extremely eloquent and percipient study of the Giscardian septennate already quoted, Alain Duhamel comments on the difficulties of the President's role as leader of a party in process of finding its personality. To succeed, he argues, a President's party (and the same must be true of an ex-President's or a would-be President's party) must be at the same time diverse enough to include as many French citizens as possible, but homogeneous enough to be able to stimulate a strong current of support. It must be democratic – but not too much so for a presidential party – a vigorous defender of the President and yet content to remain his instrument. He considered the Gaullist party to have admirably fulfilled these conditions, but added that it had all the necessary requirements for success while the UDF was, by comparison, severely handicapped – not least by the fact that its very existence was still in question.

As to how far Giscard d'Estaing has the required qualities to lead such a party, Alain Duhamel's balance sheet is subtle:

> He writes well, on the whole. He speaks even better. He does not always resist the temptation of dandyism and snobbery. But though he is credited with a taste for leisure (evidence of a balanced personality), he cannot hide his developed desire for power and his obstinate desire for influence, both for France and so for himself. . . .

Is he, then, a traditionalist? Certainly he is, but he is more than that. He has something of Disraeli and of Franklin Roosevelt. He resembles the former in his liking for the upper classes, though he has modern views on social problems. Like the latter, he is a convinced democrat, though he holds that in a country that counts and is influential innovation must be through the power of an elected executive. He is prepared to accept the theory that there are men of destiny, and would certainly not consider himself as being unworthy of being included in the list. Politically, he stands somewhere between the enlightened conservatism of Queen Victoria's Prime Minister and the wise reformism of the American President. He would like to associate the spirit of the Fifth Republic with some Anglo-Saxon political customs. Hence a courtesy and a tolerance unusual in French political circles. ... Hence the taste for intellectual debate, the desire to maintain normal relations with the opposition, a sense of the rules of the game and of social consensus, and an international outlook somewhat rare in France. ...

Hence an instinctive empiricism and a dislike for the raised voice, exaggeration and Homeric rhetoric (except, of course, at times under electoral pressure); a taste for Anglo-Saxon democracy, though not to such an extent as to persuade him to relinquish one iota of his exceptional powers.[19]

He goes on to list some of the former President's other virtues and, at times, contradictions – his desire not to attack windmills but rather to tackle serious obstacles head-on; his preference for efforts to convince rather than to impose his own points of view, a trait sometimes regarded as evidence of a lack of determination; his patience and secretiveness, combined with a relentless persistence in pursuing his objectives; his readiness, if necessary, to take risks, such as, for instance, that of creating a small party as a basis for seeking to become President in face of the all-powerful Gaullists. But – and the 'but' is one that has already been mentioned – he also saw the danger of his becoming isolated. Up to 1981 it was an isolation that could be in large part attributed to the deference that surrounds a President. But whatever the cause it left him something of an enigma for his compatriots. His septennate did not really reveal whether he was a real reformer, merely a modernizer, or an orthodox conservative with somewhat nebulous concepts of 'advanced liberalism'.

Now that the period of deference is over, the 'buts' may well prove to be among his most difficult obstacles. The election revealed a perhaps surprising degree of personal hostility to him among those on whom he would normally count for support. The emphasis on Giscardism as the *raison d'être* of the UDF could become a liability to the movement, just as its heterogeneity and centrifugal tendencies could prove an obstacle to his own ambitions to lead the non-Gaullist opposition, if that is indeed his intention. The movement, if it is still a movement, has no clear policies capable of providing an attractive alternative to Gaullism. Yet an organization, however nebulous its bonds, that could provide, along with its impressive 119 Deputies and 109 Senators, some 40 or more mayors of towns with populations of over 30,000, 8 presidents of regional councils, 32 presidents of councils of *départements* is no negligible potential political force. It remains to be seen how many of these are in reality members or associates of the major member of the UDF, the Independent Republicans – renamed since 1977 the Republican party in an attempt to efface the somewhat aristocratic image it owed to influential and titled members such as Michel Poniatowski and Michel d'Ornano. The influence of the orthodox conservative Republican party has never ceased to be important in local life, but the conventional organization of the party as one of local notabilities without a large mass membership makes it an unsuitable basis on which to build support for a national leader – as Giscard d'Estaing and his supporters realize.

In the aftermath of the presidential election, it still looks as if the UDF if it survives, or if not something like it, would be the best party (or federation) on which to base a new Giscardian leadership, and that Giscard d'Estaing would be the best alternative leader to Chirac, or whoever might lead the Gaullist party. But there would have to be adjustments on both sides. Nor should the support for the UDF between 1978 and 1981 be necessarily regarded as a permanent phenomenon. French parties have grown and declined with surprising rapidity before now and proved no less surprisingly vulnerable. The MRP was at one time the largest party in the post-war Parliament. By 1967 it had to all intents and purposes disappeared. The Gaullist party was dominant in the 1950s but fell apart when de Gaulle finally abandoned it in 1955. The Poujadist movement had 50

Deputies in 1952 and none by the following election. The most compelling reason for caution is the traditional inability of the moderate right in France to produce a large and well-organized conservative party. So far, 'liberalism', in the French sense, and whether 'advanced' or not, has always shown a singular power of resistance to the disciplines of a mass party.

The Giscardian septennate did not, then, as those who formed the UDF hoped, solve the basic problem of the right, and Gaullist and non-Gaullist elements, whether or not the latter achieves some permanent form of organization, still have to work out their relations to each other. In a climate as full of economic and political uncertainties as the 1980s promises to be, it would be foolhardy to hazard guesses as to how that relationship will develop, and even as to whether Jacques Chirac will remain at the head of the Gaullist party. At the moment, Gaullism shows no sign of finding a new source of inspiration to replace the principles formulated by General de Gaulle for a France and a world that have both radically changed since the late 1950s and early 1960s. All that can be said is that if history is anything to go by, a long period of opposition is not favourable to the creation of party unity. As has often been observed, the right's fortunes have been largely encouraged by the exercise of power, while the left has up to now felt at home only in opposition. The reversal of this situation in 1981, if it proves to be lasting, will be bound to create problems and difficulties for both.

5 The decline of Gaullist foreign policy

It has often been said that General de Gaulle's domestic policies were all, in reality, part of and subordinate to his foreign policy. His immediate successor, Pompidou, devoted much less time to foreign policy issues, and when he did discuss them aroused far less comment, either hostile or approving, and far less speculation. This was partly, though not entirely, because one of the results of General de Gaulle's foreign policy had been to close a number of doors to his successor while opening the door to increased social and economic pressures. These were politically far more divisive, and neither of the presidents who succeeded him enjoyed the particular political advantages to which General de Gaulle mainly owned his undoubted authority. These were, first, his record and personality, together with his unique style of leadership, and, second, the peculiar circumstances in which he came to power, which gave him a quite unprecedented opportunity to exercise authority. In 1958, the nation handed over to him one overriding obligation which, in its view, he alone would be able to fulfil, and so, until he had done so, he enjoyed a degree of political indispensability that few democratic political leaders have ever had in time of peace and that no French political leader had had since Clemenceau.

The fact that he did in the end fulfil that obligation, by achieving an acceptable, if not ideal, settlement of the Algerian problem, together with the peaceful and rapid evolution to independence of all of France's overseas possessions with any conceivable chance of viability as national entities, added to his personal prestige, thus helping

The decline of Gaullist foreign policy 69

him to prolong this indispensability, and to go on to carry out Gaullist policies and win support for Gaullist views in the field of foreign policy. In the climate of depressed impotence that the Fourth Republic had bequeathed to the Fifth, and that General de Gaulle had characterized as the absence of any foreign policy, the kind of comforting and heady verbal magic that he dispensed was more attractive to many Frenchmen than it would have been if it had been considered purely in the cold light of reason. In spite of its contradictions, and often its unreality, it appealed to many, sometimes for internal political reasons, sometimes precisely because it was remote from realities that had been for too long intractable, unacceptable or humiliating.

In such a climate, it is possible for very many Frenchmen to be persuaded that under Gaullist leadership France could hope to enjoy at one and the same time national independence and membership of a closely knit West European Community, of which it was destined to be the leader and spokesman; that it could hope to rely on the protection of the NATO nuclear deterrent and at the same time go its own nuclear way, even to the point of abandoning NATO while remaining a member of the alliance of which NATO was the sole expression; that it could hope, too, to become a real force in a western world dominated by the United States, and at the same time exercise a powerful influence in the countries of the potentially hostile eastern bloc.

By the time General de Gaulle resigned, in 1969, after his defeat in a referendum on purely internal matters, much of the magic had already disappeared. Some of the controversial issues were dead, some problems had been settled, and some irreversible decisions taken. The heated battles of 1960 over the creation of the French nuclear striking force had long since been forgotten, and in spite of the familiar phrases of the left included in the Socialist-Communist Common Programme of 1972, promising the cessation of nuclear production and holding out the hope of the dissolution of both western and eastern blocs, nobody in France would have wanted a government of any political complexion to get rid of the national nuclear deterrent. The debates of 1966 on France's abandonment of NATO were equally a thing of the past, and some members of the centre parties, which had been the main opponents of the decision, were by then on the eve of agreeing to enter the Government. The idea of European integration, to which the centre parties and some of the left had continued to pay lip-service during these years, was being much less talked about by those parties professing to believe in it, while the Communist party, which had originally opposed the whole European idea, had, like everybody else in France, accepted the EEC as it was, as the bulwark of French interests; the Communists' political programme demanded only the 'democratization' of the Community, without any clear indication of how or when this could be achieved.

By 1970, France's partners in the European Community also seemed to have lost any real belief either that progress towards the ostensible goal of European integration had been made or that it was likely to be made in the foreseeable future. In 1965 Couve de Murville had argued that some of the integrationist ardour of France's partners in the EEC, like some of their defence of British membership, was inspired more by the desire to find a stick to beat France with than by the intention to take any concrete steps towards supranationalism.[1] Five years later, they had dropped even the pretence of ardour. And Willy Brandt, Socialist Chancellor of a theoretically committed integrationist Germany, neither shocked nor surprised his partners when he said in 1970: 'The time when co-operation can include some supranationalism has not yet come, far from it.' Nor could they disagree when he said in 1974: 'The European Community must come to the point where it not only speaks with one voice, but also has something to say.'[2]

From 1968 onwards, a number of informed commentators and influential personalities in France were no longer trying to hide their conviction that the Community was in a state of stagnation, and that national conflicts within it were increasing rather than decreasing. None of them wanted the Community to collapse – on the contrary – but they feared that it was entering a gradual, progressive and perhaps irreversible decline. Whatever the reasons for Pompidou's decision to open negotiations on Britain's membership in 1970, they certainly did not include any expectation that Britain would galvanize the Community into renewed integrationist activity. There is some evidence that he was thinking rather of the danger that Germany's rapidly developing and prosperous economy might present to France's hopes of being the Community's dominating member.[3]

In addition to these changes, there should be added the new and depressing climate in which General de Gaulle's policy of 'detente and co-operation' with the countries behind the iron curtain now had to be carried on, in so far as it did continue to have a theoretical existence. Between 1964 and 1968 it had been the most generally popular, and certainly the most widely publicized of all General de Gaulle's initiatives in the field of foreign policy. In 1968, in spite of attempts by the General and by Michel Debré to dismiss the Soviet invasion of Czechoslovakia as 'a temporary hold-up' (*un accident de parcours*), a mere setback to the policy of detente and co-operation with the eastern bloc, it was – or ought to have been – clear to all informed opinion that the invasion was a brutal demonstration of the simple and equally brutal truth that France had all along counted for nothing in the minds of the Soviet leaders. If it were true that political attitudes are determined by logical considerations, the policy of detente would have vanished like a puff of smoke. That it did not do so was due to its popularity with the general public and especially with the left, and to the fact that, without it, the scope for anything that could be presented as an independent French foreign policy was by then seriously restricted.

By the time Pompidou became President, the focus of French foreign policy had already shifted, and it was to go on shifting. Preoccupations with NATO, defence, and the United Nations were already falling into the background. The policy of detente was reduced to a series of Franco-Soviet summit meetings followed by communiqués that were merely declarations of intent providing for measures of economic, technical and cultural co-operation. During Pompidou's presidency, France's non-participation in east-west or American-Soviet negotiations combined with the increasing pressure of internal problems, both political and economic, to make foreign policy of less interest to the general public. The personality of the President and his own political priorities intensified this tendency. For where General de Gaulle's pronouncements had often been spectacular, occasionally shocking (as in the case of the 1967 incident, and his cry of *Vive le Québec libre*), usually ambiguous and therefore controversial, those of Pompidou were, in the main, conciliatory, unprovocative, and sometimes dull.

He had, in fact, a totally different set of circumstances to contend with in the domestic field, in which General de Gaulle himself had certainly had a far less sure touch than he had had in the field of foreign policy. The 1968 'revolution of students and workers' had been a traumatic experience. It had revived fears for the political stability so recently acquired and only beginning to be taken for granted. It had left in its wake serious financial, economic and social problems on which public and government attention were both primarily concentrated. There were few foreign policy issues of interest to the public, and the second President of the Fifth Republic had not the capacity (even if he had had the will) to manufacture any, as his predecessor would no doubt have tried to do. The economic situation entailed a cut-back in nuclear production and the postponement of target dates for new nuclear weapons. European nuclear production was out of the question, for Euratom was moribund, having been brought close to collapse by prolonged conflicts between the European and national interests represented within it.

French governments were also isolated from initiatives in the international field. They objected in principle to negotiations between blocs and between super-powers. They therefore disliked the talks on strategic arms limitation (SALT), fearing that agreements might be reached over the heads of smaller powers. They disapproved of the idea of mutual and balanced force reductions (MBFR) on the ground that *uniform* reductions would weaken the relative position of the west. They also objected to such negotiations on the ground that military detente was impossible without a prior political detente. They were not, therefore, in principle opposed to the Soviet proposal for a European Security Conference on Security and Co-operation (ECSC), but mistrusted Soviet motives and so wanted to drive a hard bargain on prior conditions for their acceptance. On the basis of hopes of opportunities for diplomatic manoeuvre, leading perhaps to progress in east-west detente, they agreed to be present at the first meeting, held after a long period of preliminary negotiation in 1973. But mistrust soon replaced hopes, making France at least a moral absentee, convinced as it now was that Russia would use the organization to increase its own influence in Europe *without* necessarily making any political concessions.

These fears were consistent with traditional Gaullist suspicions of negotiations carried on at large conferences, particularly if they included the Soviet Union. They explained France's distrust of the United Nations and its refusal to attend the 1961 Geneva disarmament conference (justified by the fact that after more than 600 sessions this had achieved nothing). France had never signed the test ban or non-proliferation treaties, which it had regarded as piecemeal and inadequate alternatives to a system of general and controlled disarmament, and as having the additional demerit of impeding the defence of smaller nations more than that of the great powers.

Behind all the suspicions, however, there lay the fear that some agreement might be reached without France's having a say in it, and especially one that might change the status of Germany or weaken European cohesion, these being regarded by France, together with the permanent non-nuclearization of Germany, as the main planks in its defence against any revival of German aggression. This fear was always present – in France's relations within the Community, as well as in the wider European and international fields. For example, France approved of Germany's *Ostpolitik* so long as it appeared to be sponsored by France and so could be controlled by France, but began to fear it, as containing the threat of a new Rapallo, as soon as it became evident that Germany was now strong enough not to need France's good offices. France both feared British membership of the Community as a possible threat to Franco-German control of it and felt the need of Britain's presence as a possible means of counterbalancing Germany's growing power within it.

In the international field then, Pompidou merely continued the Gaullist policy of isolation that had been highlighted by General de Gaulle's spectacular departure from NATO. That isolation was perhaps slightly diminished by France's official abandonment in 1969 of the French strategic theory of *défense tous azimuts* (defended by General de Gaulle himself as late as 1968), and also by the existence of a greater degree of practical, if unobtrusive, cooperation between French forces and NATO organizations than Gaullists cared to admit publicly. The fact remained, however, that France was still outside the military organization on which it continued to rely for its defence, and whose forces must, in the French view, continue to be stationed in Europe for that purpose. Yet France had denied bases to NATO and would be obliged to deny adequate support in case of need, owing to the absence of all French participation in NATO co-ordination and planning bodies.

A policy of 'peace' and 'presence'

The more positive aspect of Pompidou's foreign policy was his attempt to obtain for France an enhanced status in the world, thanks to its role as a Mediterranean power responsible for trying to restore and maintain peace in the area – the policy described by his first Prime Minister, Chaban-Delmas, as one of 'peace' and 'presence'. The role of arbitrator was not a new one. It had, indeed, been claimed by Bidault, when he was Foreign Minister in the immediate post-war years, as a compensation for France's absence at that time from the councils of the great powers. General de Gaulle had given it a world dimension, along with his detente and co-operation policy. France, he claimed in a television interview during his second presidential election campaign, was alone among the powers in being on good terms with all the world. 'We have given up domination', he said, 'and are trying to promote international co-operation. . . . France alone can play this role and France alone is playing it.'[4]

Whatever in France's political experience might be thought to have equipped Gaullist France to play this role, nothing indicated that there was any willingness to accept it in the two theatres in which the President chose to operate – namely, Vietnam and the Middle East. In Vietnam, France had had no real influence for years, and in the Middle East developments during the Fourth Republic had actually diminished French influence. The Fourth Republic had seen the growth of public sympathy with Israel, partly as an expression of the anti-Germanism of the left, and partly owing to French resentment of President Nasser's open sympathies with the Algerian Nationalists. The Suez affair had been for France primarily a Franco-Israeli attack directed against President Nasser. During the Fourth Republic, moreover, France had become one of the main suppliers of arms to Israel. Under the Gaullist regime, however, the need for France to remain on friendly terms with the newly independent Arab north African states, all of which were in varying degrees anti-Israel, made it politically imperative to re-build traditional Franco-Arab relations. Since the Soviet Union was openly pro-Arab, a pro-Israeli policy might havs been held also to endanger the Gaullist policy of detente. And since the United States was no less openly pro-Israel, the influence of French anti-American sentiment could not be wholly left out of account. Thus, throughout the 1960s there was an increasing growth of trade with Arab states and of exports of arms to some half-dozen of them.

The events of the Six Day War brought out the essential weakness and contradiction of the French position. Once the warnings made by the Gaullist Government in an effort to keep the peace had been disregarded by the combatants, French policy was to try to limit the impact of the hostilities as far as possible by putting forward, on the basis of France's own non-involvement, possible conditions for a settlement. This the French Government did repeatedly, as well as restricting the supply of arms to the combatants. In January 1969, during the precarious ceasefire, the French government therefore imposed an embargo on the delivery of fifty Mirage planes to Israel (already 95 per cent paid for). At the same time a French Government spokesman objected to the Israeli raid on Beirut in terms that one could be pardoned for regarding as – to say the least – a somewhat eccentric expression of non-involvement, while some of General de Gaulle's remarks concerning Israel at this period were described by *The Times* as 'abrupt, personal, consistent and offensive'.[5]

Although President Pompidou maintained the same policy, his tone was markedly different, and his claim to a special role for France in the Mediterranean area was expressed in more modest terms. 'I would like to extend France's presence', he said. 'Since I am a realist, I intend to do this by stages, beginning, for example, with those parts of the world that are geographically close, such as Europe and Africa – whether north Africa or "black" Africa.'[6]

This statement, made to *Time* during President Pompidou's official visit to the United States in February 1970, was echoed by Ministers, and by press comment, though the latter was sometimes accompanied by doubts. But it was the French Government's action in 1970 in selling 100 Mirages to Libya which, more than anything else, made it impossible for France to be regarded as having a valid claim to 'non-involvement'. It also revealed the extent to which Gaullist governments in France were isolated from, or insulated against, world opinion, and unable to realize how outsiders would interpret their actions. The then Minister of Defence, Michel Debré, defended the transaction with vigour, offering to the National Assembly's Defence Commission a string of different explanations, some of which were both comprehensible and also defensible (though not as part of any meaningful interpretation of non-involvement). The arms, he said, were not sold to states directly involved (a weak argument, since any Arab state could intervene at any time, and Iraq, which had received arms from France, had intervened briefly); the Libyans had undertaken not to use the Mirages against Israel (a worthless undertaking, as was widely predicted at the time, and as President Sadat confirmed publicly in the course of his visit to France in January 1975);[7] it would take a long time to deliver them (an irrelevant observation in the light of the relations then and since between Israel and the Arab world). He also argued that if France did not supply arms to Libya, other powers – that is primarily the Soviet Union – certainly would (a valid argument, of course, though not in relation to France's claim to non-involvement). His argument that France needed the exports was also valid, but hardly likely to be of much comfort to Israel and its many friends in France.

As correspondents did not fail to point out, the predominant reason for the action was undoubtedly that it formed part of France's effort to restore its traditional influence in the Middle East. Disappointed Centrists, who had hoped that France's Europeanism would not permanently estrange it from its partners in the Atlantic alliance, could comfort themselves, as did Jacques Duhamel, leader of the pro-government Centrists, by reflecting that the Mediterranean was one of the rare areas in which there was the possibility of 'an independent and concerted European action'.[8] In reality, it was far too late already for the French Government's policy of 'peace' and 'presence' to succeed, if indeed it had ever been more than a pipe dream.

From 1971 onwards, Pompidou and his successor Giscard d'Estaing, were left with only three areas in which France could claim to have any independent foreign policy. It could go on cultivating Arab friendship, multiplying agreements on aid, trade and arms deliveries, and extending these activities to states of the Third World. This policy may have done nothing to increase France's influence either in the world or with the states in question, but it certainly did enable it to make arms sales one of its major exports, which strengthened its economic situation, and, when the oil crisis broke, provided a useful contribution to the balance of payments. By 1973, almost a quarter of its workers in the arms industry were concerned with exports, which, by then, constituted one quarter of its total exports of capital goods. France was already competing with Britain for third place in the arms-export business, only America and Russia being larger exporters.[9]

The second area was that of Franco-American relations. Neither President had, in fact, much elbow room, for no party in France was advocating France's return to NATO or indeed any significant modification of the policy of 'national independence', accepted from right to extreme left. Giscard d'Estaing, an orthodox conservative who had never been a Gaullist, was widely regarded as being at heart more 'Atlanticist' that Pompidou. As President, however, his majority in Parliament depended on continued support from the Gaullists, who remained the largest party, and so he did not have a free hand. Moreover, since the opposition parties failed to win the presidential election by only some half million votes and were no less opposed to Atlanticism than the Gaullists, the President could scarcely feel much optimism about the possibilities of a successful flirtation with Centrists, Radicals or non-Communist members of the 'united left', with a view to forming a more widely based government.

Pompidou did succeed in producing something of a Franco-American thaw, though a potentially ugly incident organized by pro-Israeli Americans during his American visit seemed at one point likely to defeat his efforts. But the abrasive attitude of his Foreign Minister, Michel Jobert, especially after Dr Kissinger made a proposal for a new Atlantic Charter in April 1973, did nothing to improve the climate, especially as Jobert was widely regarded as being a spokesman of President Pompidou and at one with him on all foreign policy issues. Jobert himself certainly had no doubts on that score. Questioned on his relations with the President a few days after the latter's death, he replied: 'Ma vie avec lui a été un immense accord', and this view was confirmed by the secretary-general of the Gaullist party.[10]

French-American disagreement over energy crisis

There was certainly evidence that Jobert's resistance to the American proposals for dealing with the energy problem, made at the Washington Conference in February 1974, had, as *The Times* correspondent claimed, 'flattered the jingoistic streak lurking in every Frenchman, right or left, Gaullist or Communist.'[11]

The Socialist leader, Mitterrand, described Jobert as 'one of the last intransigent spirits in foreign policy'.[12] But his own views were very similar. References in party resolutions to 'new exhibitions of imperialism', and to the 'ever stronger affirmations of the United States desire for supremacy'[13] had a markedly Gaullist ring about them. During the presidential election campaign, Mitterrand was, indeed, asked at his press conference of 2 May in what way his foreign policy differed from that of Jobert. In his reply he stressed the need for a coherent Europe which would *one day* (my italics) have the means of defending itself, the need for more vigilance in preserving Europe from the grip of multinational companies (that is, American companies) and for a French monetary policy not determined in accordance with American economic strategy. Then, after expressions of friendship and gratitude towards the United States and of France's intention to remain in the alliance until an alternative had been found, he added: 'But there must be no submissiveness! And if that is considered "awkward", then more's the pity!'

Such views were not substantially different from those expressed by Jobert after the Washington Conference:

> I think that every Frenchman wants a policy of independence for France. . . . I prefer, however, to speak of dignity rather than of independence. . . . There is no incompatibility between this demand of ours for independence or rather dignity . . . and our position. . . . I want the maintenance of American troops in Europe. That having been said . . . I must add that this is not fundamental for us, though it is for the United States.[14]

Some press comment put the position of the French Government with more brutal frankness. The director of *Le Monde*, a dedicated 'European', neither a Gaullist nor a Socialist, and never suspected of any reactionary tendencies, wrote after the Washington Conference:

> Standing alone, as in 1954, it [*i.e.* the French Government] has been ordered by its American and German allies to accept a plan under which it would be subject to the determining influence of the United States, and would be deprived of the use of the supreme weapon of economic war, petrol. Standing alone, France has once again said 'No'. . . . What is at stake is the decision as to whether Europe will or will not be Atlantic, that is to say, in reality, American.[15]

Debré's reaction was more predictable, but basically similar. 'Do the European nations', he asked, 'want to constitute an independent power, or are they resigned to the status of satellites?'[16] The comment of Pierre Pflimlin, who had been for a few hours the last Prime Minister of the Fourth Republic before General de Gaulle took over the reins, though he was a long-standing right of centre European, represented only a tiny minority opinion in a sea of Gaullist sentiments, coming equally from left and right. 'A policy,' he said, 'must be judged by its results. The results of our present policy will be bitter: an isolated France and a Europe torn apart and weakened'.[17]

The reactions to the Washington Conference did not help to improve Franco-American relations, any more than did Dr Kissinger's outburst of impatience with Jobert, in which he pointed out that Europeans could not have it both ways, that is to say, they could not develop a political relationship with the United States based on hostility, while maintaining that America must maintain its forces in Europe at their present level. The statements quoted above, and many similar ones, made it perfectly clear that that was precisely what France *was* seeking to do and believed *could* be done successfully.

The third area was the Europe of the EEC. Yet France was isolated within the Community on the issues raised by the Washington Conference, and the Community itself was divided on most of the important issues on its own agenda. The Community's weakness, as the president of the Commission, Xavier Ortoli, pointed out, was intensified by the absence of any agreed policy on monetary and economic union, or on regional policy. Now, faced with the new challenge presented by the oil crisis, it had revealed itself to be totally unable to achieve a common attitude. Commentators noted indeed that European unification had reached 'zero point'.[18] André Fontaine went further and accused Europe of going backwards. Since the coming of the oil crisis it was 'every man for himself and God for the strongest'.[19] 'When the crisit hit', said the chairman of Shell Transport and Trading, Frank McFadzean, somewhat more colourfully, 'everybody got on to their bicycles and went out to the Middle East to try and get a privileged position'.[20]

Neither President Pompidou, who was already very ill when the crisis broke and who died a few months later, nor his successor, Giscard d'Estaing, could have anticipated this situation. But it nevertheless constituted the most serious challenge that the European Community had had to face, and one that seriously threatened the future of European unification. Both Presidents concentrated their main activities in the field of foreign affairs almost entirely on action within the Community, partly because it had always been at the heart of France's foreign policy, and partly because it was by then the only remaining area in which there was any real scope for French initiatives. Both were unable to achieve any spectacular results in their efforts to strengthen the Community and to eliminate some of the pessimism about its future that seemed to be becoming more widespread in France.

Both sought specifically a leading role for France and the national prestige that success in this attempt might bring with it. In 1972 Pompidou sought to return to General de Gaulle's objective of political co-operation by proposing the establishment in Paris of a 'European Political Secretariat' – a rather pale shadow of the organization that had been envisaged in the General's 'Fouchet plans' of ten years earlier. This was quietly shelved by the European summit at the end of the year, without having really received any serious consideration.

Pompidou's other initiative, the French referendum of 1972 asking the electorate to approve British entry, had not, of course, strictly speaking, anything to do with foreign policy. Its purpose, as he himself indicated, was to obtain a resounding yes which would constitute a massive national approval of his European policy and so give him added status in the Community. It failed to do this because, in Pierre Viansson-Ponté's phrase, two out of every five Frenchmen preferred to go fishing, with the result that 39.52 per cent of electors did not vote; 17.22 voted no; and only 36.52 voted yes. In any case it committed the French Government to no action since British entry was already a fact agreed to by the whole Community. Nobody expected the French Parliament to refuse to ratify a treaty, the terms of which had evidently been highly satisfactory to France.

By all accounts, the admission of Britain was Pompidou's personal achievement; he had been reported as saying as far back as 1968–9 that if he were ever to become President, he would bring Britain in.[21] In 1969, however, he had inherited a difficult situation. What might have been intended by General de Gaulle as an exploratory gesture in the direction of British entry had led to a ridiculous diplomatic incident, the misnamed Soames affair – misnamed because the unfortunate Sir Christopher Soames was admitted by the French to have been in no way responsible for it. The consequences, nevertheless, had been a Franco-British estrangement that lasted for over a year. In any case, the long drawn-out final negotiations over the Community's Common Agricultural Policy were not completed until the end of June 1970. And since General de Gaulle had always insisted that acceptance of the CAP was a fundamental condition of Britain's membership, Pompidou, still under the shadow of the General's silent presence at Colombey-les-deux-Eglises, could hardly have done more than what he did in fact do during the first year of his Presidency, which was to stall, by imposing conditions (the famous triptych of *achèvement, approfondissement,* and *élargissement*) that Britain still had to meet before it could join. Once the first, the completion of the CAP, had been achieved, the second disappeared from French Government pronouncements, and the way was open for the third within a week.

Although Pompidou himself stated at the beginning of 1974 that the agricultural common market and the common tariff were 'the only substantial achievements of Europe',[22] it was clear that France was satisfied with the terms of British accession. For the Government's immediate reaction to Wilson's request for a renegotiation of terms that certainly no longer suited his government in 1974 was a string of official statements insisting on the impossibility of any revision of the treaty. The President himself expressed his deep attachment to the CAP and said that France must hold firmly to it, while his Foreign Minister, Jobert, said bluntly that France had paid a fair price for Britain's entry into the Community and therefore saw no necessity to pay an additional price to keep it there.[23]

Little change could be noticed in the tone of French pronouncements after the election of President Giscard d'Estaing. The new Prime Minister, Chirac, stated in his declaration of general policy that the CAP was non-negotiable (*intangible*) and that the British request for re-negotiation in itself appeared to the French to be 'irreconcilable with the fundamental objectives of the Community and also with the legitimate interests of the eight other members'.[24] It was common knowledge, wrote André Fontaine in *Le Monde*, that many people in Paris were in favour of 'an unqualified *non possumus* in reply to London's request for renegotiation, which would mean that, in their opinion, the Community could, in the last resort, do without England'.[25]

President Giscard d'Estaing's foreign policy initiatives

The President himself was more cautious. During his presidential election campaign he had expressed himself as against any substantial changes in the Treaty of Accession, but in the months following his election he did not discuss the question specifically. He did, however, take three foreign policy initiatives during the first six months of his presidency, of which the third included consideration of at least one of the requests made by Britain. The first was concerned with the energy problem. In his press conference in October, he suggested as an alternative, or possibly an addition, to the Kissinger plan, a tri-partite conference of oil producers, large consumers and importers in non-industrialized countries, adding that in any international conference Europe should be represented as a single entity. The second was a somewhat ambiguous remark about the need to 'look again' at the Community's use of the unanimity rule in the light of the practice that had grown up since 1966 after the disagreement of 1965 and the resultant so-called 'Luxembourg agreement', whose terms he described as 'incomprehensible.' Finally, he proposed a European summit meeting.

The summit met in an atmosphere of French disenchantment regarding both the state of the Community and its future prospects. Pessimistic comments had indeed been appearing in the press for the past year, stressing the priority that all members regularly gave to their own national interest and the failure of the Community to discover an identity or a function. Both the failure of the Copenhagen summit at the end of 1973 and the lack of solidarity between member countries over oil had increased pessimism about the chances of this summit's being willing to do anything to improve matters. What was needed, wrote one commentator, was not so much to revive an organization that had broken down two years earlier as to save what remained of it from further deterioration.[26] Another wrote that

> In the crumbling state in which the Community finds itself today, without a single agreed plan on anything, the President's announcement that, in the coming weeks, France will propose a

certain number of measures to revive the plan for European monetary and economic union is bold, not to say rash.[27]

The decisions taken at the summit conference were anything but rash. The President himself claimed six positive achievements. The first was the creation of a second personality for the Council of Ministers. Henceforth regular meetings would be held, at which, instead of their traditional Community hats, Ministers would wear new hats as members of a 'European Council,' whose function would be to discuss urgent political problems on which co-ordination was needed. This was a modest triumph, in that it represented perhaps a first step towards the creation of the kind of Community political organ that had been proposed first by General de Gaulle and then by Pompidou. The second and third achievements were merely requests for reports, the first (to be produced by the end of 1975) on what was meant by the concept of European union; the second (to be produced by 1976) on the conditions required for the direct election of representatives of the European Assembly. (The British and the Danes, however, refused to be associated with the second.) Neither of these decisions was impressive. To fix some future date has always been a Community method of avoiding doing anything today about a matter on which it has no real conviction that it will be able to do anything tomorrow. One example of this method was precisely the decision in 1972 (at the Paris summit of that year) to fix 1980 as the target date for European union, without having defined what was meant by the word. Callaghan, indeed, stated that he had no idea what it meant.

The fourth and fifth achievements concerned more closely the preoccupations of Britain. Agreement was reached on the establishment of a regional fund and decisions were taken on the first distributions to be made from it. This subject had been complicating Community relations for some time, and it would be over-optimistic to regard this decision as likely to prevent future quarrels on the subject. It was also agreed to create what was described as a 'corrective mechanism' to iron out anomalies in the levels of members' contributions to Community funds. This again was a decision to take action at some future date, and the proposed machinery was clearly intended to be within the existing terms of the treaty.

Finally, the President stated that Ministers had agreed to give up 'the practice of subordinating decisions on all questions to the unanimous consent of member states'. It is difficult to comment on the meaning of this decision, since the President's own statement to the press (quoted above) and the statements by British Ministers on the subject were no less incomprehensible than had been the text of the Luxembourg agreement, or compromise, the interpretation of which they were proposing to modify. It was far from clear, therefore, what exactly they had agreed to give up. Wilson informed the House of Commons that 'we said we would renounce the practice, which consists of making agreements . . . with the unanimous consent of the member states, whatever their respective positions may be regarding the conclusion reached in Luxembourg on 28th January, 1966' (*sic*), while Callaghan, spelling it out, claimed that 'those who argue that there never was a compromise are free to go on arguing that there never was a compromise. Those who argue that they reserve the right, are free to go on doing so. In that sense there has been no change.'[28] Curiouser and curiouser!

These modest achievements, if indeed they proved to be more than words, did not indicate any probability that the Community was likely to take any bold steps forward in the foreseeable future, and so the fears of those French critics who could no longer envisage Europe as the framework within which France could regain influence in the world and discover a mission, or a role, to replace that of a major power remained unallayed. Yet the idea of Europe, together with an increasingly precarious French or Community 'presence' in Africa and the Mediterranean, mainly in the form of trade agreements, were all that remained of the ambitious edifice of foreign policy built up in the minds of both government and opposition parties, thanks to the persuasive speeches of General de Gaulle. It remained the cornerstone of French foreign policy, and no party had any alternative to propose. Inevitably, therefore, something of a turning point had been reached.

It is understandable in view of France's post-war experience that this concept of a French role should have been so important. British writers have pointed out that Britain has never felt this need for general theories to justify her foreign policies. Professor James Joll has argued, for instance, that British foreign policy has been traditionally dominated simply by general moral criteria – by the concept of 'what is right' – and he quotes in defence of this view Arthur

Henderson's response to the Briand proposal for European union in 1929, which was to recommend caution, 'but cordial caution'. But Britain was not defeated and occupied in two world wars. She was able to establish a good working relationship with the United States both during and after the Second World War and so never felt the humiliation that France experienced and that was so often expressed in 'touchiness' regarding status and hostility to the United States, suspected of wishing to dominate France. France *needed* reassurances regarding her post-war status to bolster up her self-confidence during the decade of economic and military recovery, and the European idea was for many Frenchmen essentially the road back to great power status.

6 Giscardian foreign policy problems: Europe

From 1976 onwards it could be said that the President faced nothing but problems, both at home and in the field of foreign affairs. Indeed, the two fields overlapped. His position at home was made much more difficult by the now open conflicts within the government coalition, especially those concerned with foreign policy, and by the emergence of his former Prime Minister, Jacques Chirac, as the first elected leader of the Gaullist party and a widely predicted rival in the next presidential election. Although the election was then far from imminent, it was already becoming the overriding political issue on both government and opposition sides. Gaullist opposition to the President's position (real or imagined) regarding European and defence policies was therefore exploited to the full. For example, in 1979 the election of members of the European Assembly in particular afforded ample opportunities for a running battle between Gaullists and Giscardians on issues that the Gaullists were anxious to defend, irrespective of their relevance to the election in question, all parties having their sights firmly fixed on that other election due some eighteen months or more later.

The President's difficulties were also greatly increased both in internal and external affairs by the changes taking place in the world situation, and by their repercussions on defence and on the economy. There was, for instance, growing disquiet in the United States regarding the increase in Soviet armed strength and the relative weakness of NATO forces, intensified by France's determination to remain a largely absentee associate. And French interpretations of the Gaullist detente policy, as well as the French Government's policy of exporting not only arms but sophisticated nuclear equipment to a more and more disturbed Middle East, presented problems not only to the United States and to NATO, but also to France herself since her economy had come to rely increasingly on these arms exports.

The European context

Relations between the European partners did not encourage optimism either. On the contrary. By 1980, Franco-British relations were worse than they had been since Britain's first request for admission to the European Community in 1961. By comparison, the friction at the time of the so-called 're-negotiation' in 1975 looked merely like 'a little local difficulty'. In 1980, there were references to options such as British withdrawal to the status of an associate or her departure (perhaps even expulsion) from the Community. On the other hand, Franco-German relations were on the whole harmoniously cooperative, apparently justifying General de Gaulle's belief that a Franco-German axis was possible and could provide the basis for the kind of Europe he was seeking to create. But, as the post-war history of Franco-German relations had revealed more than once, it was never safe to take such appearances at their face value, and the 'little local' Franco-German incident of 1976 provided yet another demonstration of the extent to which the French continued to regard this axis with a cautious suspicion and vigilance, only too easily dominated by traditional fears and resentments never far below the surface.

The incident in question arose from a remark by Chancellor Schmidt in an interview to *Time* on 10 May in which he expressed the hope not to see Communists included in a French government. It followed a somewhat confused remark a day or two earlier, on the Bavarian television service, about Communist and Gaullist influence in France.[1] The most that could be said about them was that they displayed a not unfamiliar German insensitiveness to an only too familiar French over-sensitiveness to any remark that could conceivably be called an insult or even a slight to France. Both the French President and the German Chancellor clearly regarded the incident as trivial, and both promptly issued conciliatory statements and reaffirmed their mutual understanding.

They had reckoned without the French public's reaction. In the absence of the background to the Franco-German climate, this would hardly have ranked as the kind of small diplomatic storm in a teacup that the 'Soames affair' ought to have been in 1969 but was not owing to French suspicions of Great Britain. Only a year earlier, following the 1975 Franco-German summit meeting, the French President had stated that 'between these two very old countries, Federal Germany and France' there were 'no misunderstandings, no difficulties, but, on the contrary, a determined spirit of positive co-operation'.[2] This euphoria disappeared in a flash, giving way on the part of public opinion, if not of statesmen, to the traditional fears and suspicions of Germany that could always flare up on the slightest of pretexts but that indicated only too clearly the essential fragility of this so-called axis. Party spokesmen, one after the other, rebuked the German Chancellor; Gaullists protested against intervention in French affairs.[3] Chirac called his remarks 'thoughtless'; in July, the Socialist leader, François Mitterrand, described them as 'impudence',[4] amounting to intervention in the affairs of a partner; a leading left-wing Radical said that they amounted to 'pressure';[5] and a Communist complained that the German Chancellor had no right to speak in the name of the French Government.[6] On 27 July, there was even a demonstration in the Place de la République to protest against what was by now described as a 'Giscard-Schmidt plot' (a Communist-inspired flight of imagination).

In November *of the following year*, Le Monde stated that letters were still coming in about this incident and asked two distinguished French spokesmen on European affairs to explain why the French public was still so suspicious of Germany. The reasons they gave were very similar – fears of Germany's economic and military strength; fears of a revival of German Nazism; French memories of the occupation and of the German treatment of resisters; and French incomprehension of the German attitude to extremist movements, whether Communist or belonging to the Baader-Meinhof group. 'The simple fact is', wrote André Fontaine, that 'to a nation as divided as the French, with diversity in the blood, German unanimity is something suspect in itself.'[7]

Whatever the causes, the fact remained that the great majority of

Frenchmen shared (and still share) these suspicions. And the realization in the late 1970s and early 1980s that the hoped-for Franco-British co-operation that had been seen in the early 1970s as a counterbalancing factor to French fears of a *tête-à-tête* with Germany was not likely to materialise seemed now likely to lead to French suspicions of both Germany and Great Britain, and so to a worsening of European relations rather than to moves towards greater union within the Community. In an article, stressing what he described as France's essentially negative attitude to the advancement of European union, the well-known writer on Franco-German relations, Alfred Grosser, himself an enthusiastic 'European', suggested indeed that the influence of the permanent undercurrent of French fear of Germany constituted one of the main psychological obstacles to European union.

> If [he wrote at the end of 1978] the Federal Republic wants to advance European unity, that is seen as a desire for domination. If she is reticent, that is also proof of the desire for domination, a sign that she does not want to be bound. Whether the rate of inflation is high or low (it is low), whether real wages are lower or higher (they are higher), everything serves to demonstrate to France the danger of linking her fate to that of her neighbour within the framework of the Community.[8]

It might have been expected that in 1976 the subject of European union would be prominent on the Community's agenda, especially in view of the fact that the report on the conditions of European union, requested by the summit meeting of December 1974, and entrusted to a commission presided over by the then Belgian Prime Minister, Léo Tindemans, was published at the beginning of the year. In reality nothing could have illustrated more clearly, if illustration were needed, than did the reception of this report how little progress had been made towards the attainment of that goal, and how little could be expected in the future, especially where France was concerned. For instance, at the summit meeting in 1974 the French President (then in the chair) had undertaken to 'look again' at the ambiguities of the unanimity rule of the Council of Ministers in its revised 1966 text (briefly discussed in the preceding chapter). Nothing was subsequently heard about this, which was hardly surprising in view of the known hostility of France to any modification of the rule. Nor did mention of it in the Tindemans report give rise to any apparent interest in the subject on the part of other members of the Community. There was, in fact, very little apparent interest in the report itself, either in France or in Britain. The subject appeared on the agenda of meetings of the Council of Ministers, but by May there had been no real discussion of it, the subject having been regularly overshadowed by the wrangles over the electoral system for the forthcoming election of members of the European Assembly. The Council of Ministers, congratulating itself on the fact that the report had not been purely and simply buried, then arranged for a series of 'debates' on it, which turned out in practice to be merely a decision to hold, *at some unspecified date*, discussions of a duration of *two hours* (barely long enough for a European orator to warm up to his subject). Whereupon, by tacit consent, the report was well and truly buried.

Several comments would seem to be called for. First, it might reasonably be asked why the report was necessary in the first place, in view of the fact that at the very summit meeting that requested it all members had reaffirmed their commitment to European unity and their intention to attain it by 1980. It was clear, however, from the report on this meeting given by the British delegates to the House of Commons that they, at least, did not know to what they had been committing themselves and their country. The then Foreign Secretary, James Callaghan, said that he had had 'no idea' what the phrase 'European Union' meant, while his Prime Minister, Harold Wilson, said that he had agreed to monetary union (an objective considered by Tindemans in the report as an essential *preliminary* condition of European union, but still unattained by 1980) only as a 'long-term objective', adding that 'nobody accepted it for 1980'.[9] As to French opinion, while Ministers were committing themselves to the 1980 deadline, other French spokesmen, with considerable experience of the working of the Brussels administration from the inside and therefore presumably, unlike their masters, knowing what they were talking about, had been explaining to the French public that the Community was 'tottering' (*la chancelante communauté*),[10] and that a European currency was 'not possible in the foreseeable future'.[11]

One explanation that might well have been put forward for the unenthusiastic reception of the report was that Tindemans was known to be an ardent 'European', and that the era when almost any utopian fantasies about Europe seemed to be acceptable to French opinion was long since past. In reality, however, the report was not utopian in the sense that so much of the earlier European propaganda had been. Many of the conditions for union that it laid down were in fact very practical and were either under discussion or were specific objectives of the existing Community – the desire, for instance, for a common European stand on various international issues, the desirability of the abandonment of the unanimity rule, the need for the recognition of a European defence system – one day. Others were policies actually in process of application – the regional and social policies of the Community aiming at mitigating inequalities, for instance. Others were policies that the Community had tried (and so far failed) to introduce – like the 'snake' and the European monetary system.

In spite of these facts, the report did convey an impression of nostalgic out-of-dateness, possibly because it failed to take into account the effects of twenty years' experience of the Community's existence on the thinking of members. Whatever else it did not do, it did help to highlight the change in the European climate, and especially in France – the birth-place of post-war Europeanism – from the optimistic utopianism of the 1950s to the disillusionment and negativism of the 1970s.

Both the French and British press published analyses and comments. *The Times* (8 January 1976) concluded that the document was 'not likely to set any of Europe's rivers on fire'. French reactions included some embarrassed, laconic and predictable comment from both government and opposition spokesmen. The former Gaullist Prime Minister, Michel Debré, considered it 'Bad news for Europe, bad news for France.'[12] The Socialist leader, François Mitterrand, dissociated himself from the report's inclusion of a condition requiring the existence of a European defence system, which the former Gaullist Foreign Minister, Michel Jobert, described as 'an area of hypocrisy'.[13] In short, it was clear that the report failed to set either the Seine or the Thames on fire.

Exactly where and how did it fail to respond to the atmosphere of the 1980s? It is easier to give a negative than a positive answer to this question. Twenty years' experience of Community life had convinced its members, and France in particular, that in practice they did not want to go in a number of directions that had been part of the European dream. What progress they *had* made towards pragmatic compromise on practical issues had been made only at the cost of hard bargaining in search of a lowest common denominator. And they had been bargains, or 'package deals', in which France had shown herself to be the most determined defender of the *status quo* as defined by the terms of the Rome treaty and the Common Agricultural Policy. They had also discovered that their achievements were not bringing the conventional goals any nearer, but, on the contrary, bringing tacit if not open recognition that some of them were for all practical purposes no longer goals. For instance, it had become clear that in any foreseeable future France at least would not be prepared, whatever the political complexion of the government in power, to sacrifice a significant iota of national sovereignty or to agree to any European policy regarded rightly or wrongly by the government of any member country as being contrary to its national interests (as witness the revised formulation of the 1966 Luxembourg agreement). The determination to retain the unanimity rule in the Council of Ministers, the steadfast refusal to accept any increase in the powers of the European Commission, the unanimous French statements that an elected European Assembly must have no powers of legislative control, the refusal (even if ultimately only temporarily) to conform to a nationally unpopular ruling of the European Court – all these were practical issues fought for and won, owing to French initiatives, determination, and sometimes (as in 1966 and 1969) actual obstruction of the working of Community institutions.[14]

The evolution of the Brussels administration over these years now seemed in itself likely to constitute a major obstacle to increasing union, and indeed, to any rapid change. It had been devised to deal with the day-to-day, week-to-week, and year-to-year details of the struggles to arrive at compromises between the conflicting interests of member states. Visible evidence of its inability to do so, except at the cost of enormous waste, existed in the form of butter mountains, milk and wine lakes, deadlocks on farm prices, fish, lamb, beef . . . and so on, and at the cost, too, of the floods of multi-lingual paper-work. These were required by the thousands of Community regulations ranging from important decisions of a legislative nature to innumerable pettifogging bureaucratic rules, sometimes unenforceable, sometimes ridiculous – as for instance those concerned with such matters as the size of lorry wheels, or eggs, or the temperature of beer. By 1980, this vast, expensive and paper-logged bureaucracy in Brussels was threatened with both administrative asphyxia and financial collapse. Yet nobody knew how anything could be done about it.

It was in this atmosphere that some of the conditions laid down in the report took on the air of nostalgic out-of-dateness already mentioned. For some were merely pious hopes that could have been fulfilled at any time, if only the members of the Community had had the will or the interest to decide to regard them as 'conditions'. The condition that a European union should make itself felt in people's daily lives was clearly inapplicable, because nobody knew how to achieve it. As to that requiring European institutions to possess real powers, as has been seen, the members themselves, and especially France, were determined that they should not. The condition that European institutions should include some political powers was unfulfilled because those suggested (by France) had been consistently turned down by *all* her partners for one reason or another (for instance, the Fouchet plans, and the Pompidou proposal for a Political Secretariat with headquarters in Paris). The establishment of the European Council in 1974 – also on the initiative of France – had become a fact, but, like the Franco-German and the more recently established Franco-British summits, it was just one more organ for consultation, able to react or propose, but not to act.

What had already been evident for years in the writings of French political commentators and the silences of politicians and voters was a growing disillusionment regarding the future of Europe and even of the European Community. At the end of the 1960s, a number of knowledgeable and influential French commentators had been predicting that unless the admission of Great Britain (then under consideration by the Hague summit) could provide some new impetus, the European idea was doomed. Why it was ever felt in France that British membership *could* supply any such impetus is something that British citizens who opposed membership could never understand, for British economic interests were demonstrably in conflict with those of the Community, and especially with those of France. And even among those in Britain who supported membership, few shared the French belief that it could enhance the political status of France. Fewer still either understood or shared the European idea as it had been understood in France, with its historical background, its hoped-for contribution to the restoration of national political confidence in the difficult post-war years, and to the self-confident nationalism that the persuasive vocabulary of General de Gaulle's version of 'European Europe' added to it in the 1960s.

What the idea of European defence had meant to France during these years was something that most Britons neither shared nor accepted. It would be hard to say how far this was due to the absence in Great Britain of the obsessive fears of Germany that – understandably – have always dominated French foreign policy, and how far to the presence in Great Britain of the positive commitment of virtually the entire population to Atlanticism, as expressed in membership of the Atlantic alliance and NATO, and acceptance of the inevitable control of nuclear defence by the United States. But the fact remained that in Britain, except for a small unrepresentative section of opinion, the French version of the 'European dream' never existed. Most Britons thought of Europe in economic terms and in terms of British national interests, just as General de Gaulle, Giscard d'Estaing and Raymond Barre thought primarily of French interests. The differences between France and Britain were that French estimates of national economic benefits from membership of the Community were more accurate than those of British 'Europeans', while French versions of the European myth proved so deep-rooted that the political parties found it impossible to adapt their conceptions and their vocabulary to the changed conditions of the 1970s. Thus, the almost religious fidelity of the Gaullist party to General de Gaulle's formulations, Communist inability to modify the party's theoretical hostility to 'Europe' (even when their conduct was in complete contradiction to it), and Socialist inability to abandon the phraseology of the 1960s, all helped to make 'Europe' a concept, or rather a number of conflicting concepts, in which there were elements of partly artificial consensus and partly artificial conflict, adding up to no real European policy at all.

The future of Europe

If it was not possible to describe France's positive European objectives in the 1980s, it was at least becoming possible to discern some negative ones. When Alain Peyrefitte wrote in May 1979[15] that most Europeans had now accepted not the idea of 'confederation' – that he thought was still a long way away – but 'the confederal method', he was no longer expressing only Gaullist views but also those of the other parties as well. In his book, *Démocratie française*, published at the end of 1976, the French President, in the few final pages he devoted to foreign policy, referred, almost in passing, to France's European aims as being the achievement of European economic and monetary union 'within the terms of the treaty of Rome' (an objective that he admitted was still far from being attained) and the advancement of the confederal form of European union which, he said, could be attained 'only as a result of decisions taken by national Governments and Parliaments'.[16] When asked his attitude to federation and confederation, the Socialist leader was evasive, but nevertheless admitted that as long as the unanimity rule existed – and he was certainly in favour of its retention[17] – Europe would remain a confederation. Only the handful of uninfluential Centrists (some of them former ex-members of the MRP led by Senator Jean Lecanuet) still clung somewhat half-heartedly to the idea of federation 'one day'. Peyrefitte's claim that the European crusade was henceforth pointless, since everybody had been converted to 'the confederal idea' was therefore justified. He did not define the term, it is true, but it seemed to mean no more than the kind of loose association of nation states envisaged by General de Gaulle as the instrument that would enable France to play once again a leading role in world affairs.

If the first European objective of the 1980s was that France was *not* going in the direction of federation, the second was that she was *not* moving in the direction of a European defence system either. The report's modest suggestions on this subject were summarily dismissed by the French left as well as by the right. But the idea had long been absent from political platforms and questions about it had met with evasive negations. During the presidential election campaign of 1974, foreign policy was hardly mentioned by the two main contestants. Both paid a few words of lip-service to the European idea and summarily deferred any consideration of a possible European defence system to the Greek kalends. Giscard d'Estaing went on record as believing in 1975 that European defence was 'a problem that cannot usefully be taken into consideration'.[18]

What then remained of the idea that had for so long been at the centre of French attitudes to foreign policy? Very little. Mainly perhaps a sense of loss as expressed in the unanswered question posed by Alain Peyrefitte – 'l'Europe, pourquoi faire?' Indeed, the third negative conclusion about French foreign policy during the Giscardian septennate was that it was profoundly pessimistic not merely regarding the future of Europe but also of the Community itself. In a review of a book entitled *Sauver l'Europe* by Paul Lévy, a well-known and long-standing campaigner for European unity, André Fontaine, an equally well-known 'European' in the authentic French tradition, remarked: 'Why go on trying to create this Europe when, in one country after another, the flame is so visibly dying down?'[19] And he quoted the conclusion of the author, an enthusiast who had declared himself to be a believer in Utopia, that he shared More's own conclusion to his Utopia: 'I wish rather than hope for it.'

In an article published at the beginning of 1979 in the left-wing weekly *l'Express*, Olivier Todd commented on the mounting anti-Europeanism characteristic of the French mood at the end of the decade as being the successor of 'the anti-Americanism characteristic of the 1950s and 1960s', and of one of its principal manifestations, 'Germanophobia', a subject to which André Fontaine had himself drawn attention a month or two earlier. Olivier Todd quoted the former international secretary of the French Socialist party, Robert Pontillon, then a member of the party's national secretariat, as claiming that his party was 'still European', adding that he himself doubted this. In any case, he said, the party had clearly been losing enthusiasm over the past six months.

> In January 1979 [he concluded], the only French political movement that is clearly European is the UDF, and it is questionable whether even all its leading members are convinced. . . . Valéry Giscard d'Estaing is conscious of the absence of enthusiasm in France for the European idea.[20]

Alfred Grosser had already been deploring what he called 'anti-European defeatism' in 1978, by which he meant resistance to Community initiatives in connection with the regional fund, as revealing France's opposition to 'Community intervention' in international affairs. There was, of course, persistent Gaullist and Communist opposition to any Community activity that could conceivably be regarded as giving support to, or providing arguments for, 'supranationalism' during the campaign for the election of the European Assembly. Yet no positive picture was emerging of what was to replace 'Europeanism'. Chirac's Gaullism was purely and unashamedly nationalistic, while the Socialist party, under the leadership of François Mitterrand, seemed to be falling back on a traditional class-conscious opposition to international big business that recalled the politics of old-fashioned cloud-cuckoo land.

As to the attitude of the public, its actions spoke louder than words. 39 per cent did not even bother to vote in the European election of June 1979. The *Guardian* summed up the situation in one simple headline: 'The European dream that turned into a yawn'.

European problems

In such a political climate, the French President had little room for manoeuvre. In any case, with the best will in the world he could have achieved little while his majority in Parliament was dependent on the continued support of the Gaullist party and while no party in France, from left to right, was prepared to consider any changes in the terms of the Rome treaty and the Common Agricultural Policy. He was left, in practice, with two options, leaving aside the routine wrangles in Community ministerial meetings in support of short-term national advantages. One was to follow his predecessor's example and suggest some additions to the existing structure that involved no specific organs or powers requiring amendments to the treaties. The other was – again following his predecessor's example – to suggest a further enlargement of the existing Community of nine in the hope that France might derive some political advantage from this step. He did both in fact, by sponsoring first the establishment of the European Council in 1974 and second the admission of Greece to the Community in the early 1980s, to be followed eventually by that of Portugal and Spain.

In the light of the French campaign preceding the election of the European Assembly in 1979, in implementation of article 138 of the Rome treaty, it is difficult to regard this event as in any way advancing the cause of European union. From start to finish, and the French campaign started months before the official opening of the electoral period, French parties treated this event as a kind of opinion poll, to test their relative strengths in view of the forthcoming French presidential election, not due until mid 1981. Any European issues that arose were purely incidental in the sense that they were merely being used as political weapons in what was essentially a purely internal party political battle.

There were, in particular, three such issues. The first was the attempt by Gaullists and Communists to ensure in advance that an elected European Assembly would have no more powers than the nominated one had possessed (which meant that it would have virtually *no* powers). Gaullist and Communist Deputies sought to tie any French government's hands by obtaining a declaration in advance from the French Constitutional Council on this point (which in fact was unnecessary). The second was the attempt – again by Gaullists and Communists – to prevent 'European' interests from using the campaign as a platform for 'supranational' propaganda. And the third was opposition to any modification in the unanimity rule of the Council of Ministers (such as had been hinted at by the French President in 1974, though not apparently followed up by any action on the matter). There was, in fact, no significant difference between the four main French parties on any of these three issues, and the debate on them roused no interest except in so far as it provided fuel for the permanent Gaullist party sniping at the Giscardians, and especially at the President. Nor did the contrary plea for an extension of the powers of the Assembly, once it became an elected body, as something that 'ought to be passionately desired by many of those who are at present among its most bitter enemies'[21] carry any weight in France, where only the small band of faithful 'Europeans' – mainly Centrists represented only on the fringes of the government coalition – still shared this view.

French efforts to prevent the campaign from being used by 'supranationalist' interests did not make much sense either, except in this context of Gaullist anti-Giscardianism. In the debate in the National Assembly on private Bills tabled by both Gaullist and Communist Deputies, Debré, the acknowledged defender of the pure Gaullist word, argued that the availability of 'foreign' money for use in the campaign was unacceptable on both moral and political grounds. Chirac claimed that the campaign ought to be for 'a Europe of nations', 'as provided for under the Fouchet plans' – a singularly unconvincing argument in view of the fact that the Fouchet plans were defeated in the early 1960s by *all* France's European partners. Nor was it clear why Gaullist nationalist propaganda should be regarded as regular and legitimate whilst European 'supranational' propaganda should not. A Communist Deputy, who also condemned the use of the European election campaign as a platform for European integration, at least did so on the familiar if not convincing Communist ground that what the left called 'multi-nationals', that is international capitalist interests, were, as he put it, 'an unacceptable interference, threatening the regularity of the election'.[22]

At times, the argument became not only implausible as well as irrelevant but ridiculous, as when Chirac attacked the European Council's decision in 1974 to abandon, or seek to limit, the unanimity rule, saying that he had not realized at the time that the Government's real intention was to introduce 'a new European policy' – which was odd since he was Prime Minister at the time – and that when he did grasp this fact, it had been one of the two main reasons why he had resigned – which was even odder, since his resignation as Prime Minister took place, in fact, over eighteen months later. However, Socialist arguments were at times no more convincing, as when Mitterrand, reaffirming his own 'Europeanism', added that *his* Europe was not that of the RPR or the UDF, both of which represented 'conservative interests', but 'a Europe of workers and nations of the left' – a traditional French Socialist ideological objective, the relevance of which to the election of a European Assembly in 1979 was obscure and one that was highly unlikely to become practical politics either in France or the Community in the foreseeable future.[23] He also attacked the French Communist party for having opted out of Europe, ignoring the fact that Communists were represented in the European Assembly, and omitting to explain why, if his accusation was justified, he was still advocating a Socialist-Communist union of the left in France.

None of this party in-fighting was calculated to provide any new stimulus to European union. But hope springs eternal, and some non-French 'Europeans', among them Tindemans, were apparently counting on the creation of an elected European Assembly to do just that. So, too, was David Marquand, a British Labour MP, on the basis of an enquiry into the reasons for what he admitted to be the disappointing lack of progress towards the European goal during the 1970s, in the course of which he asked ex-Prime Ministers, Foreign

Ministers, Eurocrats, etc. for their views. Among French views expressed was that of Couve de Murville, who attributed the loss of enthusiasm to additional difficulties arising from the international monetary crisis; some believed that there had been 'a fatal flaw' in European institutions, in particular the powerlessness of the Commission – a powerlessness which France and indeed most member states were intending to retain; a former Italian member of the Commission blamed the Council of Ministers and the European Council for being dominated by national interests. Marquand thought that the European Parliament had been 'not only heterogeneous, but divergent'. Yet, like Tindemans, he was counting on a directly elected European Assembly to become 'a quite different animal from its nominated predecessor', and to be the chief instrument of forward movement. It would, he thought, show that 'it had democratic muscles to flex'.[24]

Since French opinion was unanimous in opposition to any extension whatever in the powers of the European Parliament, it is difficult to take this 'European' optimism very seriously. And if the situation of the nine did not justify any optimism, what was likely to make a Community of ten, eleven or twelve any more homogeneous or any less divergent and quarrelsome? Yet it appeared that France was seeking to create precisely the kind of Community that would be bound to be divergent (though if he had lived, Pompidou would no doubt have followed a similar policy). The French President, along with other members, had accepted the Greek request for membership, which became effective in January 1981.

During the years following the official application of Greece for full membership, doubts, hesitation, even hostility about it were evident in France and especially among Gaullists, Communists and farming interests in south-west France who were likely to be most directly affected by the decision. Why, then, was the French Government apparently prepared to agree to it and why should the prospect of Greek membership – to be followed possibly by that of Spain and Portugal – apparently create more apprehension outside than inside France? For instance, two well-known academic writers, enthusiastic students as well as supporters of the Community, spelled out very clearly what in their view would be the economic and administrative consequences of this proposed enlargement. It would entail, they said:

intense strain on the Common Agricultural Policy and the Regional and Social Funds. The Commission and the Council of Ministers would become more unwieldy and there would be even greater dilution of the Community element in EEC decision-making, rendering the achievement of meaningful common goals much more difficult.[25]

The answer is that France was not primarily seeking 'meaningful common goals', but, as she had always done – and quite openly since the beginning of the Gaullist régime – national goals, political as well as economic, in a European organization of which she believed herself to be (in General de Gaulle's words) 'the centre and the key', and which it was hoped would become powerful enough to enable Europe as an entity to regain the status of a world power. Within this framework there were secondary objectives, inevitably liable to be either incompatible or contradictory. Those concerned directly with defence are discussed briefly later. Within the Community, France's intention was to retain the dominant influence, with the help of a strong and co-operative Germany but one whose strength must not be such as to enable her to challenge French leadership. One of the reasons for the admission of Great Britain had clearly been – as Willy Brandt himself admitted – French fears of the increasing economic strength of Germany. But the admission of Denmark, Ireland and Great Britain had been regarded by France as having increased the weight within the Community of the 'Nordic' element, that is of countries regarded as likely to be more subject to German than to French influence. It was hoped, therefore, that the admission of three south European states, whose Latin culture made them more likely to be receptive to French influence, would redress the political balance.

How far this would prove to be an expensive illusion was, of course, anybody's guess. It certainly seemed to some outside observers that the chances of increased political as well as economic problems within the Community were high. All three new candidates were poor, politically unstable and with sizeable Communist parties. And though some precautions had been taken to meet the economic problems that their membership would undoubtedly pose for France – notably provisions for a long transition period leading to full membership – it was doubtful whether these could succeed in avoiding a serious increase in the economic conflicts of interest that were already threatening the Community's survival. There had certainly been miscalculations regarding the effects of British membership. It might be held, therefore, that this aspect of France's European policy *ought* to have been more of a problem than it actually appeared to be in 1979 when it seemed to be acceptable to both government and opposition parties, though the Gaullists were expected to oppose the admission of the other two south European countries.

By 1980, however, the French President was already beginning to advocate delay in admitting Spain and Portugal to membership of the Community. His attitude drew unfavourable comment from some political opponents, who reminded him that less than a year earlier he had been claiming that the entry of Spain was 'not only a legitimate aspiration, but in conformity with the nature of things and with European interests'.[26] He was criticized for having made a U-turn for purely electoral reasons, and in particular in the hope of stealing some of the electoral thunder of both Gaullist and Communist parties, which were exploiting the unpopularity of Spain's admission in the farming area of south-western France. He was also seen as using this issue to gain some electoral advantage over the French Socialist party, which approved of Spanish membership. Some opposition critics accused him of being unduly harsh on Spain. Admittedly she would seek support for Mediterranean products – and especially for olive oil – and thus increase the Community's expenditure on agriculture at a time when it was essential to reduce it. But Spain and Portugal were, they said, being punished in advance for doing precisely what Great Britain, as a member of the Community, had been allowed to do – namely, to choose her own 'narrow national interests' rather than 'continental solidarity'.[27]

This last criticism seemed to be dictated more by irritation with Great Britain than by concern for Spain and Portugal. Perhaps it was this evident irritation with Great Britain that prevented French critics from realizing that some French attitudes appeared to the British to call for similar criticism. For instance, the leader writer of *Le Monde* who put forward the above-quoted view failed to mention the 'narrow national interests' of France in relation both to imports of British lamb and to the ruling of the European Court that French policies regarding it were illegal. The commentator who described the President's apparent change of mind regarding the admission of Spain and Portugal to the Community as being dictated by 'hexagonal, viticultural, southward-looking and presidential considerations',[28] did not even bother to note the essentially 'nationalist' character of these preoccupations. And in this context it is interesting to note that Chirac's list of Gaullist candidates for the European Assembly election was presented to the press (on 2 May 1979) under the title: 'Defence of French interests in Europe.'

The one successful positive European initiative of the Giscardian septennate – the agreement in 1979 to set up a European monetary fund – was no more than a timid initial step. But it was noticeable that it was reached only after France (the initiator) had blocked its application until a compensatory measure to safeguard French national interests had been obtained, and that Great Britain's continual refusal to join was explained by the fact that Britain remained unconvinced that membership would be in British national interests.

The mood of pessimism that prevailed in France at the end of the decade, together with the tendency of French opinion to lay the blame for it on Great Britain, was well illustrated by an article (typical of many) entitled simply: 'Paris has no European policy.' Its conclusion was that

> beneath the combined blows of the crisis and of British policy, the Community seems likely to suffer a progressive deterioration. Yet a disillusioned France is allowing this to happen and making no apparent preparation for the vital negotiations on EEC reorganization that are due to begin in June 1981.[29]

The author went on to spell out the difficulties. France knew that there must be changes but could not decide what they should be. The French view was that Britain simply wanted to get rid of the CAP and had no real plan for reform. Nor was there agreement on any plan. For instance, there was no policy aiming at getting rid of the 'mountains'. One Community civil servant had commented that nobody had any ideas at all except those without any responsibilities. The French were paralysed by electoral preoccupations and not thinking beyond the yearly price-fixing. The only positive achievements were the loss of some illusions (or perhaps they were only in abeyance), such as the possibilities of European defence, a European federation and a European energy policy. Realities had become distinct from dreams.

If, as the article suggested, the future was to be that of 'the Europe of necessity' then what exactly that implied was to be a major problem for the French President in the 1980s, unless the vast bureaucracy in Brussels was to join the sad ghost of that earlier dream that failed, the Council of Europe. And if blaming Great Britain was an inadequate French response, it was no more so than was the apparent intention of half the British Labour party to opt out of the European Community, without any serious attempt to think out how such an unravelling process of the past ten years of Community history could be achieved without inflicting incalculable harm on the economies of Europe, and probably especially on Great Britain herself. Some suggestions were made by irritated French commentators in 1975, at the time of the so-called 're-negotiation', that British membership was not essential to France. Such a current of opinion could possibly be revived. For nobody had foreseen either the length or the severity of the European recession that was beginning. Even without that difficulty, it was always possible, as some critics of British membership had argued, that entry into the Community at the time and in the circumstances in which it took place might prove to be far more difficult than the enthusiasts had foreseen. Some were by no means hostile to European co-operation – far from it! But they were perhaps more familiar with the long history of French dreams of Europe that had come to nothing. As one of the most under-estimated of them once remarked in answer to a question regarding the reasons for his position: 'I am afraid that we shall reach a position in which we are unable to go forward and unable to go backward, and yet in which we cannot stay where we are.' Perhaps the most urgent problem in the third decade of the EEC's existence would be for the French Government to realize the danger that this situation could well arise unless steps are taken that, hitherto, have been prevented partly, though not entirely, by haggling over day-to-day costs and benefits. The basic problem is not the one that preoccupies Debré, that is, the need to banish the spectre of an integrated Europe. It is to enable the existing organization to survive, with all its faults, long enough to enable it to evolve into a viable international body in which national interests can be better co-ordinated. Such co-ordination would demand political as well as economic sacrifices from all members, and French governments in particular would find it difficult, and perhaps impossible, to recognize that demand. Even if they succeeded in doing so, they would probably be unable to persuade the public to accept it.

7 Giscardian foreign policy problems: defence

Though defence was not a 'European' problem, the Gaullist approach was certainly to treat it as such, if only to emphasize France's independence of the United States. But the objective of what General de Gaulle called 'European Europe' was in reality based on a fictional Europe, since it left out of account the fact that all its proposed members, except France itself, had already chosen to rely for their defence on the Atlantic alliance and membership of NATO. Instead of being the natural leader of a Europe that would include eventually some defence capabilities, France was the odd man out – or, more exactly, half out, with one foot *in* the Atlantic alliance and the other from 1966 onwards *out* of NATO.

The two main principles of Gaullist defence policy proved, however, so attractive to French public opinion that Giscard d'Estaing would have been obliged to subscribe to them. Although not himself a Gaullist, he and his party, along with both the opposition parties, accepted the need for France's continued absence from NATO and for national control of French nuclear forces (though Socialists and Communists had certainly incompatible reasons for adopting this approach). This general consensus in the field of defence also applied to the principles governing France's relations with Germany, which remained in 1974 exactly what they had been twenty years earlier. French opinion was unanimous in holding that Germany must not be allowed to become a nuclear power and that German armed forces must not be allowed to be superior to those of France. These two basic attitudes, which, under the Fourth Republic, had been described as summing up France's foreign and defence policies, were in fact incompatible with each other, constituting a doubly unsquarable circle which would have made the solution of Giscard's defence problems insoluble from the start, even if world conditions had not done so.

The Giscardian septennate was dominated by at least four specific major problems, none of which appeared to be solvable in isolation from the others, and in which military and political factors combined to prevent the necessary decisions from being taken.

One was that of the reorganization of the French defence forces themselves. Though militarily necessary, it was politically impossible. While Germany remained both prosperous and free from the burden of nuclear expenditure, it was inevitable that her forces should outstrip those of France. This was unacceptable to French opinion, and especially to the left which retained its traditional belief in the need for a large conscript army, and all the more determinedly in order to ensure military parity with Germany. The President clearly shared this view. In 1976, when Parliament voted a new *loi de programme* providing for military estimates for the next five years, he defended it on these grounds. He said: 'I consider that it is important for the military balance of our continent that French forces should not be inferior in number to those of the other continental military power, namely, Germany.'[1]

In fact, of course, they were, and were bound to remain so, as long as France's hostility to the possession by Germany of any nuclear power enabled Germany to provide not only a large conscript army but one very much better equipped than were French conventional forces. A few figures will illustrate the extent of the disparities. The 1976 *loi de programme* (the fourth since 1960) provided for some reduction in the numbers of conventional forces (though not to the point of leaving the German army with superior numbers) and for an increase in the number of tanks to 1100 by 1980. But Germany already possessed 3500 heavy tanks in 1976, and although some 100,000 more men were serving in the French forces, France was spending only half the amount spent by Germany on military equipment and training. It seemed, moreover, highly unlikely that this programme could be carried out. The targets laid down in the three previous *lois de programme* voted since 1960 had not been achieved. And a series of articles published early in 1980 by members of the National Assembly's Defence Commission pointed out serious deficiencies in both conventional and nuclear equipment which indicated that the 1976 law would meet the same fate as the three previous plans.[2]

Nor was it only the superiority of German resources that was resented in France. There was irritation, especially in the 1960s, on the ground that Germany was 'the favoured ally of the United States'. Yet this too was an unavoidable consequence of German superior conventional equipment and was reinforced by France's absence from NATO from 1966 onwards. In the absence of France, Germany was bound to be the major European partner in the conventional field. Insistence on French military parity with Germany would also certainly have been an obstacle to any move towards a European defence organization, if there had been any, just as it had created difficulties in the early 1950s at the time of the abortive European Defence Community.

There were in addition to Franco-German considerations serious internal obstacles to military reorganization, namely French disagreement regarding what ought to be the proportions between nuclear and conventional defence, and the simple fact that the country could not afford the double burden of modernizing both nuclear and conventional equipment, both of which were, as the members of the Defence Commission had pointed out, in serious need of modernization. The problem was economically, politically and militarily insoluble, as was revealed by the malaise in the army during the 1970s. Yet the reports published by the Defence Commission's members had indicated that Europe's defence was vulnerable and wholly dependent on NATO.

This background added considerably to the difficulties that would have been encountered had the President really sought to solve the second and most vital of his defence problems, that of co-ordinating strategy within the Atlantic alliance, and in particular of deciding what should be France's contribution to Atlantic defence in view of the continued determination to remain absent from NATO. The problem had been less urgent during the Gaullist decade, when the French deterrent was not yet fully in operation, when, in spite of Gaullist theories of independence, France was demonstrably wholly dependent on American nuclear power. These were also the years during which French opinion was confidently relying on the possibilities of a real Franco-Soviet detente and not anticipating the changes in the 'balance of terror' which, by 1980, had placed Atlantic nuclear defence forces in a position of inferiority to those of the Soviet Union. Nor was there any expectation of a Soviet invasion of Afghanistan that would reveal the hollowness of the comfortable assumptions in 1968 that the invasion of Czechoslovakia was an exception that could be explained away.

By 1980, it was necessary for France to decide what, in case of further Soviet aggression, was to be the French contribution to the defence of the west. The subject had been discussed before then, but official statements had been neither clear nor consistent. Allowances must be made for the inhibitions imposed by the growing political tensions of an already pre-electoral atmosphere. Competing political coalitions and parties within political coalitions were divided on defence policy, and so any definite statement on the matter would have been liable to create a political storm. In a situation in which the most powerful weapon of the two left-wing parties was to accuse each other of contemplating some degree of co-operation with a government party (thus crossing the left-right divide that still plays so important a part in political propaganda), and in which the most damaging weapons that could be used against the President were accusations that he or his supporters were contemplating co-operation with NATO or the United States, it was hardly to be expected that any decisions could be made regarding strategic problems, except perhaps under the stimulus of some immediate international crisis. Nor was it possible, even if there had been political agreement, for strategic decisions to be taken without some solution of the problems of military reorganization in France. And that in turn could not be undertaken until there was some agreement between government parties on the relations between the nuclear and conventional forces, and on which should have priority, in a situation in which resources would not permit of an adequate modernization of both.

The most striking characteristic of French statements on the subject of defence strategy, whether made by official spokesmen or by party leaders, were in fact the persistence of the Gaullist myths in what was a changed world, and their vagueness and contradictions. The attraction of the doctrine of 'national independence' seemed to have lost none of its appeal, either to the left or the right. Writing, for instance, in *Le Nouveau Siècle* in January 1980, Charles Hernu, the main Socialist spokesman on defence, objected to what he suspected might be the readiness of the French Government at that time to accept some new type of integration – a new kind of Atlantic alliance – in which each partner might have a definite role to play. He rejected this out of hand. 'We cannot', he said, 'accept any such revision, since our watchword in defence matters is the maintenance and increase of France's freedom of decision.'

What this freedom of decision was to persuade France to decide was never made clear. What, for instance, was to be the precise use to be made of the Pluto missiles which, in the latter half of the 1970s, were in service in some French units? Were tactical nuclear weapons intended purely as deterrents, or were they weapons? And if the latter, in what circumstances were they intended to be used? The answers given to these questions were both ambiguous and contradictory. In 1976 the Chief of Staff, General Méry, stated that he 'could not rule out possible French participation in the framework of allied strategy'.[3] The President referred to tactical nuclear weapons as 'an instrument of battle', 'an artillery'.[4] The Prime Minister, however, referred to them as 'a deterrent', clearly assuming that they would not have to be used. 'The problem', he said in an interview given to a German paper in 1977, 'is not to find a battlefield for Pluto missiles, but to prevent the battle from taking place.'[5] And he went on to advise his questioner not to confuse France's strategy of deterrence with that of NATO, to which France did not belong.

The question was rather whether France had any strategy at all, and if so, whether the French nation (or even the French Government) knew what it was, a doubt that the Defence Minister's pronouncements did nothing to dispel. On the contrary. He stated categorically that France ought to *avoid* any clear statement of her intentions, since uncertainty was part of deterrence. The following remarks are perhaps worth quoting:

> Our system of deterrence is, both in its conception and its means, original and autonomous. . . . The first essential is at all costs to retain our freedom of decision on the national level. Nuclear risk is not something to be shared, and France's deterrent must remain national. . . . But a precise definition of our vital interests, in terms

of place or field of action, should not be made public too soon or too clearly. Uncertainty is part of deterrence.[6]

Whether it was desirable to leave the French public, along with France's NATO allies, in this state of uncertainty might be considered to be open to question. But since official statements themselves did not seem to be in accord with each other, uncertainty there certainly was.

Defence attitudes following the Soviet invasion of Afghanistan

It might have been expected that from January 1980 onwards the changed international situation would have concentrated the attention of politicians and parties on defence problems. And indeed, a number of points of view were expressed by party spokesmen in the following months. But they did little to clarify the situation. Their numbers and variety were such as to create a third problem in the field of defence, namely that of enabling either government or opposition leaders to reach sufficient agreement to permit the presentation to the electorate in the presidential election of the following year of anything that looked like a coherent French defence policy. The problem had been avoided during the two previous election campaigns (in 1974 and 1978). Foreign policy and defence were barely mentioned in either campaign. But it was clear that in the aftermath of the invasion of Afghanistan it might well prove impossible to remain silent. Gaullists and Giscardians therefore produced party statements on defence, unsurprisingly revealing that their positions were as irreconcilable as they had been before. The statement presented by the Gaullist leader, Jacques Chirac, on 3 June 1980 emphasized the Gaullist desire to give priority to the strengthening and diversification of nuclear defence, and reaffirmed the Gaullist strategy of the massive nuclear response directed against population centres. It merely added to these targets those of decision-making and industrial centres. It retained conscription but proposed that there should be, alongside the traditional contingent of military servicemen (which Gaullists wanted to be regarded as a supportive body only), a smaller, more thoroughly trained professional army. The outline of this plan followed that of the Messmer plan of December 1967 and November 1968 included in the *Livre blanc de la défense* drawn up by Debré when he was Minister of Defence during the presidency of Pompidou. National independence and continued membership of the Atlantic alliance were simply reaffirmed.

The Giscardian *Union pour la Démocratie française* (UDF), formed before the 1978 election, approved a defence programme at the end of May 1980. It emphasized the Atlantic and European bases of defence, accepted the NATO doctrine of the graduated and flexible response and came down in favour of France's possession of the neutron bomb (which the Gaullists were rejecting as being essentially only tactical and supportive). The document was, however, no more than a reaffirmation of the position defined by the President himself in June 1976, in a speech to the Institute of Advanced Defence Studies. It also contrived to get the worst of two political worlds by using a vocabulary sufficiently 'Atlanticist' to supply both Gaullists and Communists alike with ammunition to suggest that 'Giscardisme' was merely support for NATO in disguise, yet without supplying any concrete evidence that it had anything to offer but empty verbalism.

There were also a number of party statements and speeches by political personalities on both the government and the opposition sides. For instance, Michel Poniatowski, who had been a prominent member of Giscard d'Estaing's party and a former Minister, was advocating in January 1980 the creation of a European nuclear force independent of NATO. He thought that the 'American umbrella' was now 'full of holes' and 'unlikely to protect Europe' in 'one case in four'.[7] As he must have been well aware, the President had pointed out some years earlier that 'the time was not ripe' for any European defence organization. Moreover, some of the 'holes' in American defence had been contributed by France when the decision was taken in 1966 to take France out of NATO and to deny the use of French bases to NATO forces. Nor was there any discernible support in France for the idea of European defence. Indeed, at the time that Poniatowski made the suggestion, the French Defence Minister was in London putting forward a plan for joint European production of tactical fighters, helicopters and anti-tank weapons, and running into difficulties even during the initial discussions. And Gaullist spokesmen – and especially the former Foreign Minister, Couve de Murville – were already pointing out that they found 'unacceptable' any form of collective or even intergovernmental organization of nuclear defence.

In spite of the inadequacies of French defence, both in the conventional and the nuclear field, the Minister of Defence, Yvon Bourges, advised the British public not to under-estimate the French nuclear effort, asking rhetorically whether anyone could imagine the position that France would be in without it in 1980. To nine British citizens out of ten – and to France's European partners as well – the relevant question was where Europe (including France) would be without the American defence effort, with or without holes!

Socialist statements revealed both divisions and ambiguities. The party document on defence, debated at the Socialist Convention of 24 April 1980, provided little enlightenment, while articles on defence published by leaders of different strands of opinion during the months of April and May revealed the survival of all the old divisions that it had been hoped to reconcile under the leadership of François Mitterrand following the creation of the new Socialist party in 1971. For Jean Poperen (a former leader of a left-wing minority movement, but from 1974 a consistent supporter of the Mitterrandist majority) the party's foreign policy was utterly out of date and unrealistic, with its continuing emphasis on the need to occupy some unattainable and mythical centre-ground between the super-powers described as 'national independence'. He held that this was a position indistinguishable from neutralism and made possible only by the fact that France was relying on American nuclear protection. He also thought it was a dangerous position, since it risked allowing the party to slip into the Soviet sphere of influence. For Robert Pontillon (with a long history of support for Socialist majority policies and regarded as one of the party's main spokesmen on foreign affairs) what mattered was that the party should recognize that 'Europe' no longer counted with either of the super-powers, being regarded by Americans merely as 'a kind of American province', and by the USSR as neutralist. He called for a policy of 'autonomous defence' which he suggested could avoid at one and the same time withdrawal into a narrow nationalism (*la sanctuarisation du territoire national*) and a return to NATO. Since such a policy was obviously beyond France's resources and would have had no support from France's European partners, it was impossible to regard it as anything but a familiar Socialist dream. On the Afghanistan question, he called for 'firmness' and 'flexibility', which meant in practice an effort to achieve some undefined 'negotiation' with the USSR which could be no more than a verbal formula leaving unchallenged the *fait accompli* of Societ occupation. The predominantly intellectual Marxist wing, led by Jean-Pierre Chevènement (who had been largely responsible for the *Projet de société* on which the joint Socialist-Communist programme of 1972 had been based), was even farther removed from reality, being obsessed with complicated ideological tactics designed to achieve a Socialist-led government with Communist support – which in the political atmosphere of 1980 looked like trying to square a political circle.

As for the Communist party, it remained steadfastly aloof from the whole argument, adamantly and statically anti-NATO, anti-colonial wars, anti-German nuclear rearmament, anti-European supra-nationalism, anti the French Socialist position on Afghanistan and indeed on everything else, including 'Eurocommunism' of which nothing had been heard since the breakdown of the Common Programme of the left in 1977.

In the light of attitudes such as these, it was hardly surprising that the Convention, instead of defining the party's attitude to foreign policy, produced only meaningless and often contradictory verbiage. The party secretary responsible for the report to the Convention, Lionel Jospin (one of the younger intellectuals who came into the party with Mitterrand in 1971), called for a policy of 'bi-polarization', by which he meant non-commitment to either of the super-powers and apparently also a refusal to be associated with any bloc, except of course the routine affirmation of France's continued membership of the Atlantic alliance (excluding NATO).

He also called for co-operation with the Soviet Union, in spite of Afghanistan, for the preservation of the EEC from disintegration (though by what means he did not say), for the maintenance of French interests in the Mediterranean and the Third World, and for an effort to make Europe 'more Socialist'. The members of the Convention approved unanimously a resolution on these lines – defining as party objectives the struggle against the logic of 'blocs', support for the construction of an independent Europe, for a new international order, both cultural and political, and for the rights of man and of nations. In fact, the unanimity covered some striking divergences. For example, Chevènement proposed that France should declare itself 'non-aligned' – a proposal firmly turned down. The only real conclusion was that a Franco-USSR dialogue was indispensable, though the resolution avoided actually mentioning the word 'detente'. The only clear and coherent – although unrealistic – statement came from Michel Rocard, who, after several routine calls for Europe to assert itself, for France to take initiatives (undefined), and for the reduction of European armaments, concluded that the possibilities for a French foreign policy were limited. As for Mitterrand, what appeared to emerge from his remarks was that the less said about foreign policy the better.

Though the reactions of party leaders on both sides were confused and ambiguous, it was presidential caution that came particularly under fire during these months. It was easier to express dissatisfaction with the President's handling of the situation than to produce a convincing alternative. And so the six months following the Soviet invasion saw more open criticism in press and parties, and especially by Gaullists, of presidential 'caution', 'absence of leadership', etc. What was particularly noticeable, however, was that the criticism had spread to circles hitherto noted for their attachment both to the detente policy and to France's detachment from the United States. Thus even *Le Monde*, which up to then had shared the general approval of French Government defence attitudes, found it difficult to stomach government declarations combining affirmations of the unacceptability of Soviet actions with reaffirmations of intentions to pursue the Gaullist-inspired policy of Franco-Soviet detente. André Fontaine described the French Government's decision (alone among western powers) to send an ambassador to participate in the Moscow May Day celebrations as a manifestation of Gaullism that even de Gaulle would have regarded as unsuitable in the circumstances.[8] Earlier in the year, the Government's apparent decision that it was suitable in the circumstances to *refuse* a United States invitation to a European-American conference in Bonn drew the following comment from *Le Monde*:

> a foreign policy based on principle is simple, but one that is, in the Prime Minister's words, based on national interest, appears to call for a degree of opportunism that leaves France, in effect, with no foreign policy at all.[9]

The suggestion that the refusal had been due to France's dislike of 'repeated summits' certainly did not bear examination, coming from a country which had participated in thirty-four Franco-German summits in seventeen years, four Franco-British summits in four years, a large number of unfruitful summits of the French-sponsored *Dialogue Nord-Sud* over the preceding six years and sixteen summits of the European Council.

The main ground of Gaullist criticisms of the President was that the Government's position risked giving the Soviet Union a false impression. Michel Jobert, ex-Foreign Minister and founder of the Gaullist *Mouvement des Démocrates*, accused him of being both a prisoner and a dupe by pursuing a policy of placating the Soviet Union to the point of laying himself open to charges of 'neutralism'.[10] Jacques Chirac, returning to the political stage after a silence of some months, suggested that changed circumstances demanded changed French attitudes, but refrained from offering any positive suggestions, merely reiterating France's intention not to yield either to intimidation from Moscow or to Washington-inspired policies.[11]

Two former Gaullist *éminences grises* – Pierre Juillet and Madame Marie-France Garaud – who had worked closely with Pompidou and Chirac, came out of their retirement from politics a year earlier to express their disquiet at the Government's continued defence of detente in circumstances in which it could only serve the interests of the Soviet Union. There were also warnings from outside Gaullist circles of the danger of creating the impression in the USSR that the west could always be relied on to accept Soviet policies and reminders to the French public of the consequences when Hitler had assumed that Britain would accept the invasion of Poland. Nevertheless, it remained clearly evident that the Government intended to maintain what it called a policy of 'firmness and dialogue' in circumstances in which firmness would have ruled out the kind of dialogue proposed.

It is important to remember that France was not the only western country whose reactions were open to criticism. Both British and American reactions were essentially cautious lest they should risk escalation of the existing situation into one of threatened confrontation between east and west. Statements by British spokesmen, though more supportive of the United States, were hardly more positive than those of France, while the Labour party left wing chose the 1980 Conference as a suitable time to propose unilateral nuclear disarmament! What was especially noticeable about French reactions, however, was that the dominance of the issue of the forthcoming presidential election meant that criticisms of French defence attitudes were more and more directed against the President, although, as everybody knew, he was bound hand and foot by his dependence on the support of a Gaullist and a Republican party in disagreement with each other on defence problems and equally unable to make any more positive proposals themselves. The constitutional assumption of the Fifth Republic that Presidents were in sole charge of foreign policy and defence merely made the presidential office the main target for attack and the main cause of dissatisfaction among supporters as well as opponents.

In one field of defence policy at least the President and his government were assiduously active and apparently highly successful. When President Pompidou announced in 1970 that France was going to seek to establish a 'presence' in the Mediterranean, this was regarded partly as a policy to provide some compensation to French public opinion for the disappointments caused by the failure of Europe to develop the political influence that had been hoped for, and partly to find something that could be called a world role now that the Franco-Soviet detente was losing some of the credibility that it had generally enjoyed in France. It was a myth – like the Franco-Soviet detente – in the sense that Gaullists had understood it and General de Gaulle had presented it in his campaign for re-election in 1965. It had concrete as well as political advantages. Its practical expression, when it became evident that France could play no role as an arbitrator in either the actual Middle East conflicts or the threatened conflicts, became more and more the development of the sale of arms in that area, especially to Arab countries. But even in 1970 and 1971, it raised some questions. Debré had to fight hard for the acceptance by the National Assembly of the sale of Mirages IV to Libya. Among the arguments then put forward was the likelihood of these arms being transferred to neighbouring Arab states at war. But he produced a number of cogent arguments in favour of the policy, which was in general acceptable. The sales were greatly increased, especially under the presidency of Giscard d'Estaing. At first, they were merely an adjunct to the military capacity of these states, a supplement or an alternative to exports supplied by the super-powers. Some 23 per cent of French exports were still to advanced industrial countries. But between 1974 and 1977, arms sales doubled and by 1980 France was selling them to nineteen countries in five continents, the bulk being now in the developing world.[12] Presidential visits to heads of states, mainly in search of arms markets, were multiplied to a point at which they gave rise to comment that the policy seemed to be not so much a French presence in these areas as a continuous presidential absence from France.

The visible advantages were mainly economic, the possible disadvantages political or military. Arms exports made a considerable contribution towards improving the French balance of payments at a time when the oil crisis was developing, and helped, too, to ensure France's own oil supplies. Being very labour-intensive, they helped to reduce unemployment in a period of recession. They also helped to alleviate the growing financial burden of maintaining and eventually modernizing the French nuclear deterrent and ensuring the development of the necessary technological capacity. And a not unimportant contribution was to French desires for status. Before the end of the decade, France could boast of being the third most important nuclear power – that is if Great Britain was excluded on the ground that her nuclear capacity was not independent.

The President's fourth specific problem arose from the political and military dilemmas posed by the increasing size and changing nature of arms exports. Some French fears had already been expressed as far back as 1975. For one thing, it became clear that Libya had indeed transferred some Mirages IV.[13] But the most serious disquiet arose from the proposed export of sophisticated nuclear material to Pakistan. Not only did the United States view this with alarm on military grounds, but the French Government also had a problem, namely weighing up the pros and cons if the continuance of the proposed sale were to threaten her uranium supplies from the United States. There was as well increasing criticism in France itself, and especially from the various anti-nuclear movements loosely referred to as ecologists, a term including both environmentalists and left-wing anti-nuclear movements. The demonstration in 1977 against the proposed nuclear processing plant at Creys-Malleville showed, as did electoral figures in the 1978 election, that the movement could become an electoral pressure group, a not negligible factor as the presidential election drew nearer.

There were military problems concerning the impact of nuclear production on the already difficult problem of deciding what ought to be the balance between provision for nuclear and conventional defence problems, and the political repercussions of this problem as seen in the differences between the two government parties on questions concerning defence policy. For example, by 1977 the conventional forces, though in the opinion of some too large, were receiving *under* half of the total expenditure on the armed forces.

The most serious political disadvantage was the growing realization that as the fighting and general instability of the situation in the Middle East increased, France's so-called 'presence', far from providing, as had been hoped, a contribution to peace in these areas, was an additional irritant. For it was by now clear to all that neither Israel nor the Arab states regarded France as an acceptable arbitrator, and that her neutrality was suspect to both.

Was there a Giscardian defence policy?

By the end of the decade, criticisms of the President included that directed against President Pompidou during the year preceding his death. He was described as 'merely coasting along' (*naviguer à vue*), living from day to day without any visible objectives. It was now evident that when General de Gaulle had come to his demand for a second presidential septennate in 1965, his political assets in the field of foreign policy had been considerable and his position as far as internal affairs were concerned had been incomparably stronger than that of Giscard d'Estaing in 1981. In 1965 the nuclear deterrent was only just coming into operation. In 1981 it was obsolescent and its replacement prohibitively expensive in a period of depression. In 1965 the economy was prosperous and there was no oil crisis (80 per cent of France's oil comes from the Middle East). France's position as a nuclear power was also a subject of almost unanimous satisfaction to the French public. This was the period when General de Gaulle's policy of Franco-Soviet detente as a French role in world affairs was at the height of its popularity.

In 1981 the President was facing a steadily worsening international situation in which he found himself a prisoner. His scope for action was virtually nil, while foreign policy, which had been a major factor in attracting public support for General de Gaulle, was becoming one of his main internal problems. To some extent he himself, though involuntarily, contributed to the prevailing lack of interest in foreign policy in 1980. The inability of the government parties to produce a coherent and convincing foreign policy led to the increasing tendency of both government and opposition parties to ignore the subject in their electoral campaigns. For Socialists and Communists had no real foreign policy at all. In 1974 both presidential candidates had virtually ignored the subject. In 1965 it had been a dominant issue. In 1981 Giscard d'Estaing had the additional disadvantage that he could not ignore the problem of Afghanistan yet his statements on it and on the impact of Soviet policies on the detente policy lacked conviction and, it must be added, also lacked credibility.

His own personality, too, played some part as was evident in 1976 in his references to foreign policy in the last few pages of his *Démocratie française*. His advocacy of patience and gradualism, of a deliberate attitude of 'calm and clarity'[14] – in effect the persistent attempt to 'cool it' (*je ne suis pas un président agité*) – however admirable, was not an electoral rallying call. But his greatest disadvantage was his dependence on a Gaullist party whose policy, as he himself noted, had been formulated for different times. As he said in 1974: 'Our main strategic choices were made in 1960, in a very different world.'[15] In other words, his fault was not so much in himself as in his stars. Even a de Gaulle would have found it impossible to sustain in 1981 the policies that were so successful in the 1960s. In that sense, the traditional sense of foreign policy as 'the external manifestations of political power', only the two superpowers could claim to have a foreign policy, and even then not always with total credibility.

8 The perennial problem of the presidency

Is the presidency still a problem?

In 1981, though the President had many problems, the presidency itself was not expected to present problems in the near future. The four main parties were unanimous in their acceptance of the revision of 1962, and although there were still criticisms of the extent of presidential powers, no party was proposing to make any significant changes in the existing situation. Some political commentators were advocating the revision of a few specific articles of minor importance, but there was general agreement that party and public agreement regarding the only important change discussed would rule that out.

> Unfortunately [wrote Raymond Barrillon] the immense majority of Frenchmen of all shades of opinion, on all sides, continue both to approve and to cherish the constitutional revision of the autumn of 1962. ... Since it would be very difficult to advocate the suppression of what is popular, there is not a single candidate willing to take the risk of proposing the only worthwhile constitutional revision.[1]

There was no guarantee that this relatively recent degree of unanimity would last. Ever since the Republic was created in 1875, there has been constant support for a very different concept of the presidency, though that did not prevent a good deal of criticism of some Presidents and at times of some constitutional provisions governing the exercise of the office. During the sixty-five years of the Third Republic there were two serious disagreements between President and Parliament. And a recall of the careers of the thirteen Presidents since 1875 does not convey the impression that a President's lot was a happy one. Three retired before the completion of their term of office, one because he wanted to play a more active role, the other two because they had done so and finding themselves in consequence faced with the alternatives presented to the first of them by Léon Gambetta in 1877 – *se soumettre ou se démettre* – had chosen the latter course. Two were assassinated, three retired prematurely owing to political or personal problems, one died in office; only four completed their term of office normally.

The careers of Presidents of the Third and Fourth Republics certainly suggest that the French did not think very highly of their Presidents, and were not sure either that they had yet found the kind of president they wanted. The concept of the presidential role during these years was not such as to encourage men of distinction to occupy it. Parliament almost always chose middle of the road politicians, elderly, former Presidents of either the Chamber or the Senate (as all but one were), often lawyers by training (as nine out of the thirteen were), respected but not outstanding, sometimes indeed nonentities. Which helps to explain Georges Clemenceau's well-known piece of advice in 1887: 'Vote for the stupidest,'[2] and General de Gaulle's verdict on the last of them, President Lebrun: 'Fundamentally, as head of state he lacked two things: he was no head; there was no state.'[3] With two exceptions, their functions were restricted to ceremonial duties, which, however important they might look on paper, were rendered wholly unimportant by the requirement that their acts must always have an appropriate ministerial countersignature. Even their speeches were subject to ministerial approval. The two exceptions to the rule – partial exceptions only – were, first, in the field of foreign affairs, where it was generally understood that the President did have a say in the appointment of the Foreign Minister and in some cases appointed him, and that he was able at times to have some influence in foreign policy decisions. The second was in relation to his power to choose a Prime Minister. This power could be purely formal if there was a clear majority in the Chamber of Deputies. In any case, any personal role played in the choice was still subject to its acceptance by the Chamber of Deputies. But where, as so often happened under the Fourth Republic, there were long interregna during which agreement on a new government seemed impossible, an experienced and shrewd political tactician such as Vincent Auriol could play a significant role. This possibility was clearly indicated in 1953, when it took thirteen ballots to elect his successor, René Coty; the explanation being that the bitterness over the issue of the European Defence Community and the difficulties in obtaining a parliamentary majority, made it conceivable that the choice of a Prime Minister by President Coty might influence the political balance on this issue.

The Fourth Republic started life with a controversy regarding the presidency. There was, at that time, a tri-partite government of the left, in which there was a strong current of opinion opposed to the existence of the office of President of the Republic. The Socialist leader, Léon Blum, even described the presidency in 1946 as 'A useless and inconvenient cog in a machine in which real executive power ought to belong to a Prime Minister responsible to the Assembly'.[4]

The view was not in itself new but had not before been widely held in government circles. Clemenceau, for instance, had put the same point less elegantly and more directly: 'There are two useless organs,' he said, 'the prostate and the presidency of the Republic.'[5]

The result of this current of opinion was a first draft of the constitution of the Fourth Republic providing for a figurehead even more impotent than Presidents of the Third had been. The electorate rejected this draft, and the progressive Catholics who, along with Socialists and Communists, constituted the Government managed to persuade Deputies that to allow this monopoly of power to be exercised by the Prime Minister was to risk the domination of the Government by the National Assembly – the development of *gouvernement d'Assemblé* – an accusation frequently made regarding governments of the Fourth Republic. As a consequence, the powers of the President were restored to approximately those possessed by former Presidents. The fact that the two Presidents of the Fourth Republic were highly successful had, however, little to do with their formal powers. Both held office in special circumstances – the first, President Auriol, a distinguished Socialist politician with an honourable resistance record and the first Socialist President (if Millerand, an ex-Socialist when he became President, is left out of account), holding office during the euphoric post-war years; the second, President Coty, a highly respected conservative politician, holding office during the difficult years preceding the end of the regime, who played an inconspicuous but vital role in enabling General de Gaulle to return to power by legitimate means.

The constitution of the Fifth Republic broke with the traditions of the presidency during the past seventy years. Drawn up not by Parliament but by a small ministerial committee presided over by General de Gaulle, then Prime Minister, it was submitted to the Cabinet, then to a Constitutional Consultative Committee made up largely of Deputies. It was accepted by the Cabinet and then by Parliament, and finally submitted to a national referendum. It cannot, therefore, be described as undemocratic, though the fact that General de Gaulle had made his right to control the drafting of the constitution a condition of his return to power on the breakdown of the Fourth Republic obviously raised from the start questions regarding its longevity. Politicians and political scientists predicted for years that it would survive only as long as General de Gaulle remained at the head of affairs. The office of the presidency especially came in for criticism as being alien to French traditions and an instrument of personal rule by General de Gaulle. The parties of the left, in opposition from 1959 onwards, busied themselves during the early years of the regime with plans for future constitutions including more familiar roles for presidential heads of state.

In 1959, for instance, Pierre Viansson-Ponté of *Le Monde* wrote:

> All political power has fallen from the hands of Deputies into those of one man. Since 1 June 1958, the date of his investiture, General de Gaulle has governed, and since 8 January 1959, when he entered the Elysée, he has ruled.[6]

Two years later, Professor Duverger wrote, in a book entitled *La VIe République et le Régime présidentiel*,

> Today, everybody knows that the institutions of the Fifth Republic will not outlive their creator, and that, properly speaking, the institutions of the Fifth Republic do not exist. There is only a personal consulate, which will disappear with its Consul.

Neither of these statements provided an accurate picture of the institution of the presidency. But then nor did General de Gaulle's own definition of his presidential functions, delivered on 31 January 1964 in a press conference, at a time when many of those who until then had also been dubious regarding the ability of the Gaullist conception of the presidency to survive had begun to feel that it might after all be possible that it would. As he then said:

> The President chooses the Prime Minister, nominates him along with other members of the Government, and changes him, either when he has, in his view, accomplished his allotted task, or is to be reserved for some future period, or no longer meets with his approval. It is the President who, in case of national danger, assumes the responsibility for the necessary action. The President has clearly the sole responsibility for exercising and delegating the authority of the state.

The complex and essential task of the Prime Minister, he went on, was 'to conduct the political, parliamentary, economic, and administrative affairs of the nation'. The two could not be entirely separated because if a subject of vital importance arose, then it was for the President to decide on the respective responsibilities as he thought fit. But it must be clearly understood that

> the indivisible authority of the state is entrusted to the President elected by the nation, that he is in sole charge, and that all other authorities, whether ministerial or civil, military or judicial, are appointed to and maintained in office by him.[7]

This flight of Gaullist oratory did not even represent its author's own recorded views on his relations with the Prime Minister. Therefore, before trying to assess the extent to which the office of presidency, as it exists under the 1958 constitution and as it has been interpreted by successive Presidents in practice, does or does not constitute a problem, it is perhaps worth while summing up briefly what the constitution actually lays down in the eight specific articles that allow Presidents of the Fifth Republic to take independent actions, that is without the need for a ministerial counter-signature.

To begin with, all but one are carefully hedged around with conditions of different kinds, which, if respected, impose restrictions on the President's freedom of action. The three articles which have been most criticized are articles 12, 11, 16. The first gives the President the right to dissolve the National Assembly, as Mitterrand did immediately on assuming office, and as General de Gaulle had done in 1968 in order to hold an election following the May events. The aim is clearly to seek to obtain from the National Assembly either a clear majority or an affirmation of where the majority stands, as for instance after the disturbances of 1968. The use of the power is limited by the provision that the President cannot again have recourse to dissolution for a period of twelve months. Any President is therefore bound to weigh up carefully the pros and cons of using this power in order to ensure as far as possible that he does not make his position more rather than less difficult. It should also be added that the power does not give him any right to carry out any action of his own, but merely enables him to hand over to Parliament, in other words indirectly to the electorate, the responsibility or the power to act.

The second (article 11) gives the President the right not, as is often loosely stated (and as General de Gaulle himself sometimes stated), to decide to hold a referendum, but to accede to a request for him to do so made either by the Government or by the two Houses of Parliament. If the conditions are strictly adhered to, it gives him no right to take action on any matter, but merely asks the electorate to decide the question. Also, the subjects of such a referendum are few and narrowly defined. The question must be to approve a government Bill concerning the organization of the public authorities, or to approve a Community agreement, or to authorize the ratification of a treaty affecting the working of institutions. Again, no independent presidential action is concerned, only the approval of government actions.

The third (article 16) is really in a category of its own. It concerns only a period of serious crisis constituting a national emergency, when the President may take over the power to run the country. Again, his use of this power is limitatively defined. He must first consult the Prime Minister, the Presidents of the two Assemblies and the Constitutional Council, and inform the nation that he has done so. He must also consult the Constitutional Council on the measures that he takes. Parliament has the automatic right to meet in these circumstances and may not be dissolved. All the measures taken must be inspired by the desire to restore the situation to normal with the minimum of delay.

This article aroused more discussion than all the rest put together.

The safeguards were more clearly here open to abuse because there is no requirement that the President shall follow the advice of those whom he is obliged to consult. Nor is there any machinery for assessing whether everything that the President does on the authority conferred by the article is solely concerned with the crisis and the measures to resolve it. A great deal of legal and constitutional argument has been carried on on these points. But it is not strictly relevant to the consideration of past presidential behaviour, because on the only occasion that the article was brought into play, in 1961, on the occasion of a military revolt in Algeria, the fears expressed about its abuse proved to be unjustified. The President restored normal government after five months. There were some relatively minor criticisms as to whether all the 'decisions' taken were strictly relevant to the conditions of the crisis, though there was no serious accusation of excessive use of the powers, or of any presidential tendency to prolong the powers unduly. However, the provisions themselves created a number of unexpected administrative or legal problems, which indicated that Presidents might in future hesitate to have recourse to them unless it was absolutely essential.

Of the remaining five powers, only one has had any real political importance. The other four concern the President's duty to accede to a request by either the Prime Minister or the majority of the members of the National Assembly for the right to meet in special session to consider a specified agenda (article 29); the President's right to deliver messages to Parliament, which must be read for him and are not subject to debate (article 18); his right to nominate three of the nine members of the Constitutional Council (the other six being nominated by the Presidents of the two Assemblies, each of which chooses three) (article 56); his right, along with the Presidents of the two Assemblies, to submit laws to the Constitutional Council before their promulgation (article 61).

The use of the fifth power, however, did arouse considerable criticism. Article 8 (i) gives the President the right to appoint the Prime Minister (which his predecessors had during the two previous regimes) and to terminate his period of office on the presentation by the Prime Minister of the Government's resignation. There is no mention in the article of his right to terminate the Prime Minister's period of office if he has *not* resigned – in other words, to dismiss him, as all three Presidents did at least once.

How far do presidential constitutional powers constitute a problem?

Although presidential recourse to at least three of these powers was criticized as involving a degree of unconstitutionality, only in the case of two did any actual problem appear to have arisen. There were a few minor allegations of irregularities in the actual procedure applying article 16, but in general it did not create any real uneasiness. On the contrary. But this was intended to be used only in exceptional conditions of national peril. General de Gaulle's five referenda were criticized on political grounds, namely that the request for one yes in reply to two different questions amounted to political pressure. But, as the electorate demonstrated on the last occasion, the remedy was in its own hands. In 1969, it resisted this pressure and defeated the President, bringing about his resignation. There were criticisms of the President's habit of announcing referenda before he had complied with the constitutional requirement that he had only the right to *accede* to a request for a referendum made by the Government or Parliament. The situation was in fact always eventually regularized, as the following example shows.

In announcing the referendum of October 1962, he said: 'The President of the Republic may submit to the country any government Bill – I repeat any government Bill – concerning the organization of the public authorities, to be voted by referendum.' In his message to Parliament a few days later, he said: 'In deciding, in accordance with the Government's proposal of a Bill to this end (i.e. constitutional revision), I judged this to be the best way to make the appropriate changes.'[8] The constitutional requirements had thus, if somewhat belatedly, been respected. What was perhaps criticizable, though not unconstitutional, was his inaccurate description of himself as having the right to propose a referendum, and, in the case of the use or misuse of article 8 (i), as possessing powers that he had earlier expressly denied that he possessed. His statement of 31 January 1974 has already been quoted, claiming his right to choose the Prime Minister and dismiss him. But in 1958 he was questioned on this precise point by the Constitutional Consultative Committee:

> *Chairman* (M. Paul Reynaud): The second question concerns the Prime Minister; he is appointed by the President of the Republic. Can he be dismissed by him?

Prime Minister (General de Gaulle): No! For, if that was so he could not effectively govern. The Prime Minister is responsible to Parliament, and not to the head of State.[9]

Here again, however, the constitution was always formally respected, since Prime Ministers widely known to have been dismissed had in every case obligingly resigned (not excluding Chirac in 1976).

The only problem of substance concerned the presidential use of the referendum in 1962 to revise the constitution, which the majority of the Deputies held to be unconstitutional, article 89 having laid down the procedure for constitutional revision, the first stage of which was a vote by the two Houses of Parliament. The National Assembly, therefore, defeated the Government on this issue, and the President of the Senate formally submitted the Bill to the Constitutional Council for its verdict under article 62.

Though both the referendum and the general election resulted in a victory for General de Gaulle, the institutional problem could not be resolved, since the constitutional definition of the Council's functions rendered it incompetent to pronounce on the matter in dispute. It remained, therefore, a potential source of future conflict between President and National Assembly.

The importance of these presidential constitutional powers is twofold. First, some of them did cause political controversy, and others could if a situation existed in which a President and the parliamentary majority were in disagreement. In particular, article 11, if used in ways that Parliament refused to sanction, could oblige a President to choose between withdrawing his attempt to use the referendum, or, if he felt that his policies were being thwarted, resigning and causing a presidential election, possibly at a politically delicate moment. And second, the two main left-wing parties never regarded them as desirable presidential functions. Both the Socialist programme of 1972 and the Common Programme had proposed to revise the constitution in order to abolish presidential powers used without a counter-signature (articles 11 and 16), to prevent constitutional legislation by referendum and to reduce the presidential mandate to five years. The Socialist Manifesto of January 1981, largely drawn up by Mitterrand, promised only two constitutional changes directly affecting the presidency, the reduction of the mandate to five years (with the possibility of a second term), or, if it remained at seven years, its restriction to a single term, and the abolition of the President's right to appoint members of the *Conseil supérieur de la magistrature*. But it also promised an institutional change that would no doubt affect him indirectly – the restoration of proportional representation – and added an instruction that the constitution must be strictly applied where relations between Government and Parliament were concerned (no doubt referring to the independent powers that had been in dispute) and a promise to submit the revisions proposed in the Socialist programme to Parliament.

The new septennate

François Mitterrand's immediate decision following his victory in the presidential election – to dissolve the National Assembly – removed (at least for the time being) three important potential presidential problems. What had been the longest electoral campaign of the Fifth Republic (the 1981 election dominated political interest for almost the entire septennate) was followed by the unprecedented Socialist victory after what must have been, if not the shortest, certainly the least eventful general election campaign (for a Socialist victory was generally taken for granted). The new President had, therefore, reason to hope that for five years he would not have to contend with either a legislative or a presidential election and so might be spared the demands made by the electoralism that his predecessor had to endure. Second, he could reasonably hope not to encounter opposition to his policies in the National Assembly, in which the Socialists had a comfortable overall majority and did not need to depend on the support of any other party – also an unprecedented situation during the Fifth Republic. And third, for the first time in French Republican history a Socialist party was, numerically at least, in a position actually to put into practice policies that successive generations of Socialists had held to be the essential step towards the transition from the existing system to Socialism.

In the immediate future, the new Assembly could expect to see the by now familiar 'bipolar quadrille' replaced by the more normal confrontation in parliamentary democracies between government and opposition. For the time being the Communist party was shackled by the responsibility of office, even if only to the extent of holding four portfolios of minor political importance, and the diminution of its parliamentary representation was such that it had little power to harass or embarrass any government. On the other side, the disarray of the UDF, while perhaps providing Chirac with a possible opportunity to consolidate his position as unchallenged leader of the opposition forces, was not such as to make possible either a continuation of anything like the Chirac-Giscard hostilities that had existed for the past five years or a continuation of anything like a united opposition front.

In spite of these advantages, the political situation promised to be very difficult. The President was facing not only all the problems that had been unsolved during the Giscard d'Estaing presidency, but also all the additional problems that would be created by the introduction of the promised Socialist measures in a climate of unprecedented economic recession and gloom both in France and throughout western Europe, which included France's main potential customers. There was no ground for believing that a government of any political complexion held the key to a solution of existing economic problems or could improve the situation in the Middle East (which included France's main customers for arms exports and her main suppliers of oil) or could affect east-west relations. But there was some ground for anticipating political difficulties within the President's own party. Perhaps also within the imposing team of presidential advisers, most of whom had been trained in the same schools as those of the preceding President and might well have more in common with their bureaucratic predecessors than their political masters when it came to implementing Socialist policies in detail.

That being said, it would be unwise to exaggerate such difficulties, for it is often forgotten how much more control in France is normally exercised by the permanent civil servants under any regime, whether Socialist or not, than is the custom in Great Britain (or at least was the custom when local government authorities were less closely controlled from Whitehall). Nevertheless, it might well be that if the most cruel commentary on the right's position was made by Jean-François Revel when he said 'Giscard has succeeded in losing an unlosable contest,'[10] the most pertinent question for the left, once the initial euphoria had worn off, would be: has Mitterrand really won an unwinnable victory?

Among the first of the President's tasks was that of demonstrating to public opinion that something significant had changed. He set the stage both before and during the electoral period by seeking to create an impression of orderly and speedy changes of policy in areas in which he was free to act without having recourse to Parliament. Thus, the first and second Council of Ministers announced a batch of social and economic measures including, for instance, increases in the minimum wage, family allowances and old-age pensions; measures to help the unemployed; forthcoming discussions on other problems, such as the position of farmers and small businesses and the need for changes in the educational system; the decision to set in motion studies on worker participation in industry and the decentralization of French administration, etc. Statements by newly appointed Ministers, and in particular the Finance Minister and the Prime Minister, contributed towards the hoped-for creation of a government image of energetic but practical and moderate action.

He had also to make clear to the public what exactly in his view he had been elected to do, and this he did even before the election, in the communiqué following the Council of Ministers meeting of 3 June, in which he said that 'The undertakings made by him during the presidential campaign, and approved by universal suffrage on 10 May, constituted the charter of governmental action. These undertakings must be honoured.'[11] In his first speech, on 9 June at Montelimar, he spelled out some of the implications of this statement. It meant, first, that he considered himself bound by these commitments, no more and no less. In other words, neither the Socialist Project nor the Manifesto was to be regarded as part of government policy, though some of the commitments of the Manifesto were in fact reaffirmed during the campaign. It meant, second, that his first priority would be social and economic measures, the first instalments of which had already been announced. 'We have', he said, 'started the battle for employment.'

On 3 June an agreement was reached with the Communist party on measures dealing with unemployment, steps to deal with the problem of the young unemployed, and on negotiations regarding the improvement of working conditions – the introduction of a shorter working week and an extra week of paid holidays, the lowering of the retirement age, an increase in the minimum wage and family allowances, measures to help the old, the handicapped, women, the young and immigrants, on means of introducing more worker participation, on the democratization of the public services, decentralization and the introduction of proportional representation for regional elections, etc. In the light of experience of previous Socialist-Communist agreements, a specific statement was to be issued regarding areas of agreement and disagreement. It was significant that the areas of disagreement included issues of foreign policy.[12]

The list was impressive, and in so far as it would help to prevent Socialist and Communist controversies regarding these policies, undoubtedly useful. But it had to be remembered that many of the subjects mentioned would be bound to involve long and difficult negotiations regarding the details of implementation, time scales and so on. For as yet the agreement was largely only on general principles.

Some possible presidential problems

Among the specific commitments of the electoral programme, there were two institutional changes and a somewhat vaguely worded promise of a third. The first was the reduction of the presidential mandate to five years, with the possibility of a second term, or alternatively, if the mandate remained at seven years, its restriction to a single term. The second was a promise to introduce proportional representation, both in national elections and in regional assemblies and some municipal councils (excluding small villages). The third was a promise to extend opportunities to use the referendum.

All of these could involve problems for the President. For instance, what would be the effects of a change in the presidential mandate? Would it lead to a reduction in the electoralism that had consumed so much time and effort during the past septennate? Would it lead perhaps to an extension of presidential importance, as Professor Duverger had argued in a book written at the beginning of General de Gaulle's presidency?[13] He believed that as it stood the 1958 constitution was not viable and that if President and Assembly were both to be elected for a five-year term, this would inevitably lead to the eventual merging of the functions of Head of State and Prime Minister, and the establishment of a presidential instead of a parliamentary system (or, as he saw it, an inefficient and partially parliamentary system). Or would it, as Giscard d'Estaing believed, actually increase the importance of the presidency in the existing system?

> It is undeniable that a long period of office is necessary; even seven years is too short a period in which to complete programmes that have been introduced. This is so in the case of the multiple warhead missiles or of French electro-nuclear production. But it is equally undeniable that in a number of fields there is a constant expression of a society's desire for renewal. Several questions are therefore involved.... If the length of the mandate is reduced, the fact must be faced that the effect would certainly be to increase the strength of presidentialism in the country. And if France were to have a presidential election every five years, it is clear that the sole influence on political life would become that of the President of the Republic.[14]

The restoration of proportional representation was acceptable to both Socialist and Communist parties. It had certain practical advantages, for instance, the elimination of gross inequalities between *départements* with very small and very large populations. The *département* of Lozère, for instance, with an electorate of just over thirty thousand required only about twelve to thirteen thousand votes to elect a Deputy, whereas that of Essonne, with a population of over 181,000, needed six times as many votes. What might prove in practice a problem for a Socialist President was that it would certainly favour the Communist party, as compared with the existing system. It has been calculated that at present a party which receives 32 per cent of the votes can be virtually certain of obtaining a majority of seats, as General de Gaulle did in 1962. With a system of proportional representation, 32 per cent would obtain only one-third of the seats.[15]

One problem that could perhaps be created for Mitterrand was that proportional representation might tempt a minority movement at present within the party to stand independently, especially if it became dissatisfied with the rate of progress towards Socialism, as might well happen. For one query suggested by the President's announcement regarding the limitation of his commitments is the possible effect that it will have on party attitudes. He may not find it as easy as he anticipates to ignore documents that have after all been accepted by a party conference as official Socialist programmes. It is easy to understand why the President should want to forget about the Socialist Project. It was described by David Watt of *The Times* as 'A programme of such antediluvian far-left orthodoxy that Mr Arthur Scargill and Mr Ted Knight could stand shoulder to shoulder without the slightest discomfort'.[16] But so could many rank and file French Socialists, who for twenty-three years had nursed dreams of Socialism and 'the rupture of capitalism'. So, too, could members of Chevènement's CERES movement. Chevènement had indeed been largely responsible for the drafting of the Socialist Project. Might not one of the reactions of a sizeable minority movement in a large majority Socialist party be more rather than less militant, especially as there had been during those years no pressure on the Socialist party to restrain minority-mindedness? In such circumstances might there not be a tendency even to seek separate representation under a proportional system?

Nor would the CERES and like-minded Socialists be likely to forget that the Socialist Project had been recommended to them by Mitterrand himself at the party conference that voted for it. The gist of it was, he said,

> First, the idea which has never ceased to inspire a century and a half of working-class struggle, the ever-new idea of a classless society from which the causes of exploitation of man by man will have been eliminated, in particular by the transformation of economic structures and industrial relations.[17]

Marie-France Garaud, during her brief period as a would-be presidential candidate, had described Mitterrand as being 'still shackled by his previous agreement with the Communists'. Might he not find himself now, once the honeymoon period was over, shackled by some members of his own party, and in particular by those who still hankered after an understanding with the Communist party? This question has been touched on briefly in relation to Socialist-Communist future relations. But the attitudes of the Communist party itself could well constitute a presidential problem, whether or not they also affected those of the left-wing elements of the Socialist party. For it would be naïve to suppose that the partial electoral eclipse of the Communist party in 1981 could be counted on to persist indefinitely. And the comfortable assumption apparently being made in some circles that four minor ministerial posts would ensure Communist respect for collective responsibility of Ministers and support in the National Assembly by the fifty or so Communist Deputies or by the rank and file of the party in the country was certainly not justified by past experience. The brief period of Communist participation in government in 1974 – which, it must be remembered was a time when Socialist-Communist relations were far more amicable, when the party was far larger and more influential, and hopes of eventual re-unification were still not finally abandoned by the rank and file of the Socialist party – provides some salutary information that should perhaps be kept in mind. After a period of months only, the first Prime Minister of the Fourth Republic, Paul Ramadier, was obliged to dismiss Communist Ministers who had opposed government policy on some issues on which the entire parliamentary party had voted against the Government.

One problem that could be counted on to stimulate traditional Communist opposition to governments would no doubt be provided by discussions on how to pay for the announced social and economic measures. Early estimates provided no real clue as to the scope of the problem or to the adequacy of the proposed resources to deal with it. But experience showed that Communist representatives were traditionally ready to come to the defence of (small) taxpayers and that opportunities were, sooner or later, bound to present themselves, when the familiar habit of Deputies (whether on the right or the left) of keeping their social principles and their wallets in separate pockets reasserted itself. It would therefore be an illusion to believe that the Communist party could not, perhaps within a period of months, become an active opponent of what it recognized as unpopular measures of taxation. The struggle in the National Assembly during the first years of the Fifth Republic to reduce or suppress the privileges of small home distillers (*les bouilleurs de cru*) will be remembered by many students of French politics, as will the role played by the Communist party in that controversy.[18]

The President and technocracy

Another possible presidential problem concerned the promise to decentralize and debureaucratize the civil service. There had been during the last years of Giscard d'Estaing's presidency mounting criticism in the press of the increasing numbers and growing influence of senior civil servants both in government departments and especially in the Elysée.

With the development of presidentialism, the problems of bureaucracy have been intensified in two ways. Under all three Presidents, but especially during Giscard d'Estaing's septennate, there were criticisms of increased presidential control over the administrative machine by means of a network of administrative committees directly controlled from the Elysée. To some extent this development was logical and inevitable. The more the President rather than Parliament became the focus of political interest as well as the real directing power of the Government, the more responsibility was bound to be attributed to him if things seemed not to be going well. And the more extensive the so-called 'presidential sector' became, the more presidential organs grew up to make and carry out policies and the less Parliament exercised its ostensible role of controlling governments through debate, informing the public and maintaining its interest in the political process.

This development was encouraged by several things. First, Parliament under the Fifth Republic met for two sessions only lasting in total under six months, and one of the sessions was almost wholly taken up by debates on the budget. There were fewer votes rousing political interest since governments were to all intents and purposes no longer threatened by defeats in Parliament. The process of debate itself had less drama about it because institutional devices such as the 'block vote' and the inability to defeat a government without entailing a general election ensured the passage of government Bills. And in spite of denials of the existence of a 'presidential sector' on foreign policy issues, the decline of interest in foreign policy was a natural development of the President's *de facto* control of it and of the existence of a wide field of national consensus regarding foreign policy.

With French economic development and modernization, the growing emphasis on modern technology led to an increasing need for high-powered administrators and industrialists, not only in government departments but also as heads of nationalized and state-aided industries, and in defence and nuclear fields. And France possessed a number of excellent training colleges able to supply the need.

It was fashionable under the Fourth Republic to blame the unstable and shifting parliamentary majorities for the domination of the civil service – or alternatively to claim that only the existence of such a powerful and stable administration prevented the political system from collapsing. Under the Fifth Republic, it could be claimed that if the country were to keep up with the pace of modern economic and technological developments, a highly qualified administration was essential. And the strength and influence of the administration was further increased by the fact that the stability of governments permitted closer co-operation between Ministers and their civil servants, while the domination of a single political party protected officials from the pressures of competing rival parties.

Under the Fifth Republic, there was, too, an increasing tendency, which originated with General de Gaulle, for Presidents to prefer civil servants to professional politicians in ministerial posts, and especially as Prime Ministers. These in turn staffed their *cabinets ministériels* with increasing numbers of civil servants rather than political nominees. There thus grew up what was described by critics as a 'power elite' in which Ministers, technocrats and administrators, trained in the same colleges and with the same social and intellectual backgrounds came to constitute a kind of separate estate of the realm. *La République des Députés* had, it was said, become *La République des fonctionnaires,* or *des Grands Commis*.

Researchers into this recent development of French centralization and bureaucracy have produced some convincing figures to bear out this view. To begin with, whereas, as has been said, Presidents of the Third and Fourth Republics had (with one exception) been professional politicians, all three of the Presidents of the Fifth Republic belonged to the new ruling class. General de Gaulle was a product of *St Cyr* and the *Ecole de Guerre*; Pompidou was a *Normalien*; Giscard d'Estaing was a product of three of these schools – *Polytechnique*, ENA and the *Inspection des Finances*, and had had a long career as Minister of Finance. Of the twenty-two members of his last government, fifteen were high civil servants, not politicians. A third of the members of governments of the Fifth Republic were senior civil servants who had become Ministers, while another third were ex-civil servants, and 90 per cent of their personal advisers – the members of the *cabinets ministériels* – were chosen from one or other of this small number of products of exclusive and intellectual state training colleges. 'The Council of Ministers', wrote Alain Duhamel in the chapter of his *République giscardienne* on Giscard d'Estaing's septennate, 'came to look more and more like a meeting of civil servants.'[19]

Leaders of political parties also often belonged to the same 'club'. On the majority side, five at least of the leaders of the Gaullist party did; and on the Socialist side, the main leaders in the news, Rocard, Chevènement, Jospin and Joxe, were all products of ENA. A list of forty-two of Mitterrand's close advisers published in the weekly press just after his election makes instructive reading. A number of these had more than one of these qualifications, but counting only one for each member what emerged was that six were *énarques*; four were *Inspecteurs des Finances*; eight were lawyers or highly qualified in law studies; three were specialists in economics or industry; two were historians; one was a *Normalien* and one a *Polytechnicien*; seven were women with varied qualifications in politics, journalism or secretarial fields, and they included one member of the *Conseil d'Etat*; ten had varying qualifications more directly relevant to political functions, such as experience as mayors, local government officials, trade unionists, and they included one specialist in defence questions.[20]

The President's problem in relation to this development arises from the fact that so many critics of the Government during the last years of Giscard d'Estaing's presidency expressed their frustration by focusing on this aspect of his governments. Since the development is bound up with the exercise of presidential power that all parties now support and seek to possess, the victorious candidate is bound sooner or later to encounter similar complaints and to be asked what he is going to do about the situation.

Something of the possible effects on the presidential image of these criticisms can be gauged from the following examples taken from the political press during the last year of the Giscard septennate. 'The public', wrote Charles Hernu, one of the President's forty-two advisers, 'accepts with resignation the reign of the experts.'[21] Madame Marie-France Garaud, a former close adviser of Pompidou, wrote: 'From 1974, France has been governed by technocrats,' and in a later letter to the press she referred to 'a cohort of irresponsible technocrats, very pleased with themselves and their expertise'.[22] An article in *Le Monde*, entitled 'l'Election du Roy', claimed that

> The characteristic of the régime is the personalization of power. ... Everyone knows that the French Government is run from the Elysée Palace and that the Prime Minister is no more than a civil servant. There is no longer only one 'reserved domain'. All state business, important or unimportant, belongs to it if the President decides to take an interest in it. Absolute power has become the rule and the democratic use of power is the exception.[23]

In a chapter devoted to this aspect of Giscardism in the book already quoted, Alain Duhamel concluded that

> The French executive is a Government and civil servants serving a President and a Prime Minister who are ex-civil servants, surrounded by personal assistants from the same 'grandes écoles', and dealing with civil servants with the same background as theirs.[24]

In the 1920s and 1930s, the left had opposed the grip on the state machine of what were described as 'the two hundred families'. By the 1980s the 200 had become 5000 or more, and some put the figure at nearer 10,000.

In so far as the President himself feels this development to constitute a problem he is faced with two questions, neither of which is easily answered. The first is not whether or not he should do anything about it, but whether he *wants* to do anything. For he is the main beneficiary of the system, and the difficulties of the presidency as it has developed are such that he needs all the resources he can command. The second is whether, assuming he wants to do something, he *can* in reality do anything. It has been suggested in a recent American study of the French administrative élite that its present importance is largely due to a combination of three characteristics of the political system under the Fifth Republic, namely, presidential power, a stable majority in Parliament made up in the main by members of a single dominant party, and the consequent growth of closer relationships between political and administrative representatives. The last-mentioned is most clearly evident in the increasing tendency of Presidents to appoint civil servants to ministerial posts, and of civil servants to move from administrative to political posts, whether in the Government or in the legislature, and then to return to their administrative positions or move to positions in industry. If this is so, then the extent to which the functions of civil servants and politicians have been and are being merged creates a situation that must be in the short run irreversible. And all the more so as it has always been the case that French administrative training colleges have produced a large number of top executives to fill posts in business as well as in governments.[25] Only a return to weaker Presidents and stronger Parliaments could reverse the process, with the attendant danger of a return to the former domination of the Government by the legislature and to unstable political majorities.

Reflecting on the present situation, the *secrétaire perpétuel* of the *Académie des Sciences morales et politiques*, Bernard Chenot – himself an ex-Minister, Vice-President of the *Conseil d'Etat*, and member of the Constitutional Council – in his annual report made a number of suggestions to remedy the problem of presidential domination of the permanent executive. They included a reduction of the presidential mandate along the lines proposed by President Pompidou and now being proposed by President Mitterrand; the requirement that the President should have the assent of the Senate in order to use his power of dissolution of the National Assembly; the restoration of the parliamentary right of *interpellation*; and the substitution for the vote of censure (which to be successful requires the votes of a majority of the members of the Assembly) of a vote of confidence (which requires only a majority of those voting). The advantage of these changes would be, in his view, that they could be introduced by a procedural change without requiring a revision of the constitutional text – that is, except for the change in the presidential mandate.[26]

The first observation regarding them that springs to mind is that they involve precisely the procedural devices that political parties used to bring about frequent defeats of governments of the Fourth Republic. If, of course, as President Mitterrand has stated, he intends to restore proportional representation, which would increase the number of parties and so render the majority of a single party less probable, then the stage would be set for a return to the situation that the Fifth Republic's constitution was largely designed to get rid of. The result might well be an increase in the number of professional politicians in the Government as well as in Parliament, and so of increasing the competition between them to establish close relations with the administrators. But the process would be hazardous and slow and its effects on centralization and bureaucracy incalculable.

Moreover, the process does not take into account the principal obstacle to its acceptance, namely the refusal of all parties at present to consider any reduction in presidential power.

This refusal has been explained by the survival in France of the nostalgic desire for a leader – 'a father with the authority to dominate our disorders and silence our contradictions'[27] – but whatever the reasons the existence of the obstacle is an undisputed fact.

One question that arises in connection with the generalization of complaints during the last years of Giscard d'Estaing's presidency of presidential and bureaucratic domination is why it should be more resented in 1980 than it had been in 1970. It was, after all, General de Gaulle who encouraged the appointment of civil servants as Ministers, and who treated both with equal ruthlessness. That fact perhaps helps to suggest an answer to the query. In their discussion of the governmental process, the Webbs stated that civil servants ought to be 'on tap, but not on top'. This was precisely what both administrators and Ministers visibly were during the Gaullist era. Giscard d'Estaing was possibly regarded as being too obviously a member of the administrators' 'club' to be their master. Another explanation is perhaps General de Gaulle's position as having twice assumed power in a period of national emergency, together with his ability as a master of words able to persuade his compatriots that, with him in power, the world role he envisaged for France would be achievable. Holding office in a period when France's opportunities to play a world role were demonstrably few, and without General de Gaulle's charismatic qualities, Giscard d'Estaing had fewer assets and the domination of officials was perhaps more obvious.

The image and the man

Both of General de Gaulle's successors clearly felt themselves to be at a disadvantage in following him and both tried to create a personal image. Pompidou began by trying to establish more contact with the public – to create an impression of being merely one Frenchman among others – but abandoned this approach when he was made to realize that the Elysée is not a suitable décor for simple citizens and that the French would prefer it to remain that way. On one occasion, when he had given an interview, informally wearing a pullover and *espadrilles*, the press comment was that he looked 'rather too much like the average Frenchman on holiday'. Giscard d'Estaing's initial experiments in the role described by one critic as that of 'Monsieur-tout le monde devenu président'[28] were even less happy, and were either disliked as affectation, resented as being patronizing or dismissed as 'gimmicks'. Presidential styles in press conferences and interviews differed widely. General de Gaulle liked well stage-managed ceremony, appearing centre stage flanked by serried ranks of Ministers. Whether delivering a set speech or more informally answering questions put by journalists, his style remained formal, but he made use of a number of evocative phrases, of occasional flashes of sardonic wit or even of slang. His familiar sallies – directed at political parties, European enthusiasts, the United Nations in particular – together with a certain lofty detachment and at times ambiguity, combined to make the occasions talking points, often for weeks. Pompidou was an eloquent speaker, with authority, able to hold interest with the occasional erudite allusion or quotation and also to stand up to numerous questions from journalists, most of which were not known in advance and to which he provided genuinely impromptu answers. Giscard d'Estaing's elegant and well-ordered dissertations, full of impressive facts and figures, made a less effective public appeal, and one particular (and rare) flight of verbal fancy fell very flat indeed. Concluding his inaugural address as President in 1974, he said:

> *De ce jour date une ère nouvelle de la politique française. . . . Voici que s'ouvre le livre du temps avec le vertige de ses pages blanches.* [Today is the beginning of a new era in French politics. . . . The book of Time lies open, with the exhilaration of its blank pages.]

He was never allowed to forget this, even in summaries of his septennate in 1980. It was described in the press as being 'naively literary', 'a bold cliché', and dismissed as affectation along with some of his early gestures. Such points are no doubt petty, but they are part of the stuff that the images of public personalities are made of, especially in the French political press, where high-level commentators abound and intellectual and literary standards are demanding.

Giscard d'Estaing's more political qualities or shortcomings have already been mentioned in an earlier chapter, in relation to his contribution to the concept of 'Giscardism' and the prospects of his possible future as a party leader in what might prove to be a long period of opposition. For the time being, however, it is the personality of the incoming President that will monopolize the interests of press commentators. Is there a Mitterrandist image? No question is more difficult to try to answer as yet. No French political personality is more elusive. He is certainly a talented orator, with a literary flair that should enable him to avoid possible pitfalls. His own inaugural address was a model of elegance, brevity, sobriety and political suitability, with its keynote of hope and idealism. His combination of political subtlety, the ability to reconcile adversaries in the most unpromising circumstances (he has claimed to be *un rassembleur*) and to appeal to large and enthusiastic audiences has so far served him well in the ten years during which he has successfully led and steadily increased the national appeal of what must be one of the most difficult bodies on earth to control – the French Socialist party. Among his personal qualities are persistence (if not obstinacy), patience and tactical skill; a sense of the continuity of French Republican history, and of French Socialist history, in which he sees himself as the heir of Jaurès and Léon Blum; a recurrent need for solitude and reflection in the French countryside and the companionship of books; a consuming interest in history and poetry, rather than in Marxism or economics. He is a writer, something of a stylist. All these characteristics do not really add up to a personality easy to classify. Nor do his attributes as a Socialist politician. He appears traditionalist rather than modern, indisputably of the left but not the far left; uninterested in ideological subtleties. As a leader he attracts loyalty rather than hero-worship and his methods have been described as combining ruse, guile, prudence and the flexibility of a trapezist with calculation, touchiness, modesty, reserve, distance, reflection and boldness, ambition and ambiguity . . . to which could be added, apparently, an incurable unpunctuality!

These characteristics, if their attribution to him is accurate, present a very different image from that of his predecessors. The Gaullist presidency was one of great ambitions but of political dangers and difficulties, of economic progress and prosperity, of parliamentary stability but of constitutional speculation and uncertainty. The Pompidolist years provided political and constitutional stability, but foreign policy disappointments and threats of economic difficulties ahead. Giscard d'Estaing had hoped that his septennate would be a 'time of happiness'.[29] Instead, it was one of difficulties and disappointments both in the economic and the foreign fields. It ended in an atmosphere of public disillusionment and of considerable personal unpopularity. Mitterrand saw his victory as the victory of hope – hope of a new alliance of Socialism and liberty and of a country that would be a true national community at peace with all, and he pleaded for national confidence and faith in the future. He will need plenty of both these qualities, whether or not his 'Brave New World' ever sees the light of day.

Notes

Chapter 1: The significance of the Gaullist decade

1. *L'Année politique* (Paris: Presses Universitaires de France, 1965), p. 456.
2. See *Le Renouveau* (Paris: Plon, 1970), pp. 15, 179, 212, 254. See also Alfred Grosser, 'L'Anti-Américanisme en France', *L'Express*, 4–10 September 1978, and Guy de Carmoy, *The Foreign Policies of France (1944–1968)* (University of Chicago Press, 1970), p. 478.
3. *Notre République*, 10 November 1967.
4. Jacques Fauvet and Jean Planchais, *La Fronde des Généraux* (Paris: Arthaud, 1961).

Chapter 2: The problem of electoralism

1. *Le Monde*, 5 January 1981.
2. Jean Charlot, *Le phénomène gaulliste* (Paris: Fayard, 1970), pp. 64–6.
3. Expressions used by Chaban-Delmas in a speech of 29 January 1970 on institutions.
4. *L'Année politique* (1979), pp. 97, 109, 110.
5. See comments in *Le Monde* (19 November 1979) on presidential visit to Midi-Pyrénées.
6. See, for instance, *L'Express*, 22 March and 12 April 1980.
7. *Le Monde*, 25 May 1979.
8. Criticism by André Laurens in 'L'Action diplomatique du Président de la République', *Le Monde*, 4 May 1979.
9. ibid.
10. Interview of 1 June 1979.

11 Alain Duhamel, *Le Monde*, 12 July 1979.
12 Jean Rey, *Le Monde*, 23 July 1979.
13 André Fontaine, 'Le Décalage', *Le Monde*, 28 June 1979.
14 The 'affaire' of the diamonds cropped up again and again in the press, as did (though to a lesser extent) the suicide of Boulin at the end of October 1979. The President was asked questions on both in his broadcast of 27 November 1979. On 16 January 1980 *Canard enchaîné* published an alleged income tax demand for the President. Brief summaries are given in *L'Année politique* (1979), pp. 109–10, 122–3.
15 The President said (broadcast of 27 November) that he would not have recourse to the law of 1881 which protects the President from personal attacks of this kind and others. General de Gaulle invoked this law on 118 occasions, and President Pompidou did so 17 times. Giscard d'Estaing did not do so at all.

Chapter 3: Problems of the left

1 For a brief account of the failure of the attempt, see Dorothy Pickles, *French Politics: The first years of the Fourth Republic* (London and New York: Royal Institute of Foreign Affairs, 1951), pp. 23–9.
2 In a statement to the Paris press on 22 February 1973, Paul Laurent interpreted this commitment as being renunciation 'immediately' of the French nuclear force, the reconversion of industry, the reduction of the period of military service, and steps to achieve French independence of all military blocs whatsoever. Questioned, he added that the Communist party would close the bomber bases of the Mirages IV and the sites of strategic missiles. This statement is in direct contradiction with the statements in the Common Programme (pp. 171–2) regarding an agreed timetable and (p. 174) the undertaking that the dissolution of the Atlantic treaty would take place simultaneously with that of the Warsaw Pact.
3 Quoted in *Le Monde*, 17 February 1973. He had also put forward this condition at the previous meeting of the Communist Central Committee in January 1973: 'It is necessary that the Communist party should be the strongest party on the left.'
4 Quoted in *Le Monde*, 7 November 1972. Other Socialist statements reiterated this condition, e.g. Georges Izard (*Le Monde*, 23 January 1973).
5 Television interview of 12 February 1973. This undertaking was repeated in *Le Défi démocratique*, by Georges Marchais, published in September 1973.
6 See Georges Marchais, programme *Cartes sur Tables* (Antenne 2, 23

148   Problems of Contemporary French Politics

   March 1981), in which he appeared to be threatening direct action to bring pressure on the Socialist party – e.g. references to the intervention of workers 'par la lutte' and 'le soutien des masses' to bring pressure to bear on the Socialist party.
 7 The Séguy 'petite phrase', made in an interview in February, reported in *Le Monde*, 20 February 1973, repeated at the *Fête de l'Humanité* the following September, appeared to recommend 'des luttes ouvrières' aimed at creating a climate in which the left could win power. It was the earlier occasion on which Olivier Guichard made his comment (*Le Monde*, 20 February 1973). But the phrase was still being talked about in October.
 8 See press conferences of Pompidou on 21 September 1972 and 9 January 1973. See press conference of Giscard d'Estaing of 22 April 1976.
 9 Qualification made by Mitterrand at a meeting on 14 February 1973.
10 At the party Congress of that year in Paris.
11 Thierry Pfister, in *Le Monde*, 16–17 February 1975; Raymond Barrillon, *Le Monde*, 12 February 1975. Barrillon stated in the article that for the past four months Communist attitudes towards the Socialists had been perpetually abusive.
12 In the *Evening Standard*, 23 January 1976.
13 Reported in *Le Monde*, 16 October 1980. Ellenstein added that the Communist position in 1980 could certainly not be described as Eurocommunism, but was rather 'archéo-Communisme'.
14 Statement made at the Socialist Convention at the end of January 1980.
15 See article 'Le Choix socialiste', *Le Monde*, 26–7 October 1980.
16 In article 'Pourquoi', *Le Monde*, 3 February 1981.
17 'La révision apparente', *Le Monde*, 11 April 1978.

Chapter 4: Problems of the right

 1 *Political Parties and Elections in the French Fifth Republic* (London: C. Hurst & Co., 1977), p. 27.
 2 These nine included: the *Club Nouvelle frontière*; the *Mouvement pour le socialisme par la participation*; the *Amicale parlementaire*; *Présence et action du Gaullisme*; the *UJP*; the *Union travailliste*; Edgar Faure's *Comité d'Etudes pour un nouveau contrat social*. Among the movements which refused to be associated with the nine was the *Association d'action pour la fidélité au général de Gaulle*.
 3 Remark made by Pompidou on 21 February 1973.
 4 Quoted in *Le Monde*, 17 December 1974. Couve de Murville was by then converted to the view that the party could not go on as 'les godillots du pouvoir', but must become a party. Messmer was still calling for a

rassemblement, expressing solidarity in the service of France. To which *Le Nation* replied: '*Rassemblement* about what, and solidarity with whom?' Michel Jobert was still running an independent *rassemblement* of his own, really a kind of lone Pompidolisme! By 1975 the overwhelming majority of the party representatives at the *Conseil national* were supporting the leadership of Chirac. Internal quarrels were beginning to die down.

5 *L'UNR: Etude du pouvoir au sein d'un parti politique* (Paris: Cahiers de la FNSP, 1967), p. 23.
6 Jean-Noel Bergeroux in *Le Monde*, 24 December 1980.
7 Daniel Seguin, *Les Nouveaux Giscardiens* (Paris: Calmann-Lévy, 1979), p. 36.
8 Speech of 11 September 1980 (quoted in *Le Monde*, 13 September).
9 *Le Monde*, 13 September 1980.
10 Seguin, pp. 7–8.
11 Alain Duhamel, *La République giscardienne* (Paris: Grasset, 1980), pp. 194–5.
12 Said by Olivier Guichard in article on the President in *Le Monde*, 15 November 1980: 'Vers la fin du Parlement'.
13 Speech of 9 May 1979 at Villeneuve-sur-Lot.
14 In a television programme on Antenne 11 (*Une heure avec le Président de la République*), 18 April 1979.
15 Comment by a journalist on the programme of 5 May, *Une heure avec le Président de la République* (*Le Monde*, 7 May).
16 Noel-Jean Bergeroux in *Le Monde*, 20–1 May 1980.
17 *Le Matin*, comment on letter from the President to Raymond Barre. Also criticized in *Le Figaro* and *La Nation*. The last two emphasized the pointlessness of the gesture since most of the measures referred to as outlining the Prime Minister's future programme had already been voted on, or at least been decided on. *Le Matin* described the letter as a typical presidential gesture, a 'pedagogic exercise' in which he addresses the Prime Minister 'like a teacher talking to the best boy in the class' (*Le Monde*, 15 November 1980).
18 Article by André Laurens, 'Le Discours et la réalité', *Le Monde*, 19 April 1980.
19 Duhamel, p. 246.

Chapter 5: The decline of Gaullist foreign policy

1 Debate in the National Assembly, 18 June 1965.
2 Interview in *Le Monde*, 31 January 1970; statement made in the Bundestag, 24 January 1974.

3   See, for instance, Willy Brandt's assumption that this was so, quoted in Uwe Kitzinger, *Diplomacy and Persuasion* (London: Thames & Hudson, 1973), p. 71.
4   Television interview, 14 December 1965.
5   *The Times*, 8 January 1969. On 1 January the General had condemned Israel for 'actes exagérés de violence'.
6   *Time* magazine, 14 February 1970.
7   *The Times*, 30 January 1975.
8   *Le Monde*, 29 January 1970.
9   ibid., 15 and 26 January 1974.
10   ibid., 17 April 1974. Sanguinetti had confirmed the accuracy of this view earlier (*Le Monde*, 21 February 1974).
11   *The Times*, 23 February 1974.
12   *Le Monde*, 20 June 1974.
13   See text of resolution voted at the Socialist party Congress, quoted in *Le Monde*, 24 and 25 March 1974.
14   ibid., 10 and 11 March 1974, report of broadcast on Europe I.
15   ibid., 15 February 1974.
16   ibid., 16 February 1974.
17   Speech at the Lille Rotary Club, quoted in *Le Monde*, 22 February 1974.
18   *Esope*, January–February 1974.
19   *Le Monde*, 23 January 1974.
20   Quoted by John Lambert in *The Sunday Times*, 27 January 1974.
21   See André Fontaine, obituary in *Le Monde*, 4 April 1974.
22   Radio interview, 23 January 1974.
23   Reported reply to Callaghan, quoted by Maurice Duverger, 'Les Protectorats d'Europe', *Le Monde*, 3 April 1974.
24   Declaration of general policy 5 June 1974. These sentiments were reaffirmed in September. See *Le Monde*, 2 September 1974.
25   'L'Europe entre l'axe et le triangle', *Le Monde*, 18 June 1974.
26   Leader in *Le Monde*, 3 September 1974.
27   ibid., 29 August 1974.
28   Statements in the House of Commons, 16 and 19 December 1974.

Chapter 6: Giscardian foreign policy problems: Europe

1   A brief statement of this incident is given in *L'Année politique* (1976), p. 197.
2   Communiqué of 3 February 1975, and President's statement on television of 4 February (report in *Le Monde*, 6 February 1975).
3   Brief report in *L'Année politique* (1976), pp. 234–5.
4   ibid.

5 ibid.
6 ibid.
7 André Fontaine, in 'Ombres sur le Rhin', *Le Monde*, 9 November 1977.
8 Alfred Grosser, 'Le défaitisme anti-européen', *Le Monde*, 13 December 1978.
9 Statement to House of Commons, 16 December 1974. Reported in Hansard for that date.
10 See, for instance, Paul Fabra (*Le Monde*, 29 August 1974), who refers to 'l'état d'émiettement où se trouve aujourd'hui la Communauté des Neuf'; see also Jean de Broglie, President of the Foreign Affairs Commission of the National Assembly, who described it in 1971 as 'virtually a ruin' (*Le Monde*, 12 October 1971). There were many such statements from 1969 onwards (Dorothy Pickles, *Government and Politics of France*, vol. II (London: Methuen, 1973), pp. 260–4; also Marjolin Report of the European Commission, published in April 1975.
11 Article by Jean-François Deniau, 'Nécessités américaines et vérités européennes', *Le Monde*, 20 October 1971; see also leader in *Le Monde*, 3 September 1974, describing the Community as 'pratiquement en panne depuis au moins deux ans'.
12 Interview by Michel Debré on *France-Inter*, 8 January 1976, also *Lettre de la Nation* for the same date.
13 *L'Année politique* (1956, p. 156) quotes this remark, together with a number of other French criticisms.
14 For a brief summary of this boycott of the Community for seven months see Dorothy Pickles, *The Uneasy Entente* (Chatham Essays, Oxford University Press, 1966, pp. 57–62). For a detailed account of the controversy and the boycott see John Lambert, 'The Constitutional Crisis 1965–1966', *Journal of Common Market Studies*, May 1966. For a brief account of the fifteen-month boycott by France of the WEU Council of Ministers in 1969 see Pickles, *Government and Politics of France*, vol. II, pp. 250–3.
15 In a review of *De l'Europe de la raison à celle du coeur* by Jean Castarède, *Le Monde*, 25 May 1979.
16 Valéry Giscard d'Estaing, *Démocratie française* (Paris: Fayard, 1976), p. 163.
17 Mitterrand interview during the electoral campaign for the European Assembly (*Le Monde*, 1 June 1979).
18 See interview of 3 May 1974 during the presidential election campaign, where he was clearly assuming that any attempt to organize a European defence system was a long way off.
19 *Le Monde*, 25 May 1979.
20 *L'Express*, 13 January 1979.

152 Problems of Contemporary French Politics

21 Alfred Grosser, 'Le défaitisme anti-européen', *Le Monde*, 13 December 1978.
22 Ducoloné, Communist Deputy, in the National Assembly, 11 December 1978.
23 Statement of Mitterrand to journalists of 23 May 1979.
24 David Marquand, 'Europe: the distant dream', *The Listener*, 20 March 1980.
25 Geoffrey Edwards and William Wallace, *A Wider European Community*, Federal Trust paper, November 1976.
26 *Le Monde*, 7 June 1980.
27 ibid.
28 Bernard Chapuis, 'Au jour le jour', *Le Monde*, 7 June 1980.
29 Philippe Lemaître, 'Paris n'a pas de politique européenne', *Le Monde*, 25 November 1980.

Chapter 7: Giscardian foreign policy problems: defence

1 Speech of 2 May 1976. Some of the material in this chapter was included in the article 'The political imperatives and dilemmas of French defence policies', first published in October 1978 in *West European Politics*. This was a special issue on *Conflict and Consensus in France*, and was later published in book form (London: Frank Cass).
2 See articles by the UDF Deputy Arthur Paecht on the obsolescence of French defence (*Le Monde*, 7 November 1979) and three articles by members of the National Assembly Parliamentary Commission on Defence (a) on the need for the modernization of the French nuclear deterrent and financial inadequacies; the need for a neutron bomb, for a strong navy with better nuclear equipment and for more tactical nuclear weapons; (b) on the vulnerability of Europe, the weakness of NATO and the absence of any common defence policy other than reliance on NATO; and (c) on the absence of either tactical or strategic planning and the lack of any evidence of the will to tackle these problems (*Le Monde*, 8, 9 and 10 February 1980).
3 *Revue de défense nationale*, June 1976.
4 Speech of 1 June 1976 at the *Institut des hautes études de Défense nationale*.
5 Interview of 3 August 1977 in the magazine *Stern*. Also *Le Monde*, 4 August 1977.
6 Speech at Avord (Cher) in July 1976. Quoted in *L'Année politique* (1976), p. 236.
7 Article in *Le Monde*, 29 January 1980 reporting the broadcast on this theme.

8   Article in *Le Monde*, 8 May 1980.
9   Michel Caste, 'Au Jour le Jour, Intérêts', *Le Monde*, 10–11 February 1980.
10 *Le Monde*, 5 February 1980.
11 *Le Monde*, 15 May 1980.
12 Figures given by Edward Kolodziej in 'France and the arms trade', *International Affairs*, January 1980.
13 Revealed by President Sadat during his visit to France in January 1975.
14 Giscard d'Estaing, New Year message, 1981.
15 Press conference of 25 July 1974.

Chapter 8: *The perennial problem of the presidency*

1   Raymond Barrillon, article on 'République et Monarchies', *Le Monde*, 27 January 1981.
2   Quoted in Adrien Dansette, *Histoire des Présidents de la République* (Paris: Amiot-Dumont, 1953), p. 73. The remark was said to have been made before the election of President Sadi Carnot (later assassinated) and became a stock joke, repeated in connection with the elections of Presidents Loubet, Fallières – and even Poincaré!
3   Charles de Gaulle, *Mémoires*, vol. III, *Le Salut*, chapter on 'La Libération'.
4   *Le Populaire*, 23 August 1946.
5   Quoted in Dansette, p. 276.
6   *Risques et chances de la Vème République* (Paris: Plon, 1959), p. 1.
7   *L'Année politique* (1964), p. 421.
8   ibid. (1962), pp. 675, 677.
9   *Travaux préparatoires de la Constitution, Avis et Débats du Comité consultatif constitutionnel, La Documentation française* (séance du 8 Août, 1958), p. 118.
10 *L'Express*, 16 May 1981.
11 *Le Monde*, 5 June 1981.
12 *Le Monde*, 6 June 1981.
13 *La VIe République et le Régime présidentiel* (Paris: Librairie Arthème Fayard, 1961).
14 Interview of 27 February 1981 to *Figaro* magazine.
15 Figures quoted in *L'Express*, 29 May. A communiqué published by the Communist party on 15 June estimated that the party could have counted on upwards of eighty seats if the election of 14 and 21 June had been held under a system of proportional representation.
16 *The Times*, 15 May 1981.

17 Extract from Mitterrand's presentation of the document to the Socialist conference at the end of January 1980.
18 See account of this in Philip Williams, *The French Parliament (1958–1967)* (London: Allen & Unwin, 1968), pp. 85–8.
19 Alain Duhamel, *La République giscardienne* (Paris: Grasset, 1980), p. 63; see, in particular, statistics given in the chapter entitled 'Les Cinq Mille'.
20 See list of members of Mitterrand's team of advisers in *L'Express*, 22 May 1981.
21 *Le Monde*, 9 April 1980.
22 Letters to *Le Monde* of 20 November and 16 December 1980.
23 Jean-Denis Bredin, *Le Monde*, 18 November 1980.
24 Duhamel, p. 65.
25 Ezra N. Suleiman, *Politics, Power and Bureaucracy in France: The Administrative Elite* (Princeton University Press, 1974), see chapters 13 and 14 of part IV.
26 Report of Bernard Chenot for 1980 to the *Académie des Sciences morales et politiques* (quoted in *Le Monde*, 2 December 1980).
27 Jean Denis Bredin, *Le Monde*, 18 November 1980.
28 Quoted by Léon-Jean Bergeroux in the article on Giscard d'Estaing's presidency in *Le Monde*, 20–1 May 1980: 'Six ans après l'élection de M. Giscard d'Estaing'.
29 ibid.

Index

Académie des Sciences morales et politiques, 141
Afghanistan, 41, 109, 111–19
Algeria, 1–2, 11, 25
Arab states, 74–5
arms exports, 76–7, 87, 118
Atlanticism, 38, 49, 94
Auriol, Vincent, 123
autogestion, 31–2, 36–7, 45

Barre, Raymond, 11, 21, 56
Barrillon, Raymond, 37, 57, 121
Bidault, Georges, 74
'bi-polarization', 18, 114
'bi-polar quadrille', 17, 130
Blum, Léon, 30, 44, 123
Bokassa *affaire*, 20, 25
bouilleurs de cru, les, 136
Boulin, Robert, 53
Bourges, Yvon, 113
Brandt, Willy, 70, 101
Briand proposal, the, 85
British foreign policy, 84–5
British Labour party, 29, 104

Callaghan, James, 83, 84, 90
Capitant, René, 6
Catholic Popular Republican movement, 29–30
Centre des Démocrates sociaux, 57
Centre d'Etudes de Recherches et d'Education Socialistes (CERES), 36, 46, 135
Centre national des Indépendants et Paysans, 58
Centre républicain, 58
Centrists, 48, 55, 57, 76, 95
Chaban-Delmas, Jacques, 10, 16, 19, 22, 49, 50, 53, 74
Charlot, Jean, 15, 54
Chenot, Bernard, 141
Chevènement, Jean-Pierre, 45, 114, 115, 135
Chirac, Jacques: CAP, 81; defence, 111, 116; European Assembly, 21, 22, 98–9, 103; future of the right, 66–7; Gaullist party, 52–3; Giscard d'Estaing, 10, 53–9; presidential election, 86; resignation, 15, 50; UNR, 48
civil service, the, 136–42
Clemenceau, Georges, 122, 123

Coluche, 25
Common Agricultural Policy (CAP), 10, 11, 81
Common Programme, the, 31, 34, 38–40, 41, 44–5, 56, 129
Communist party: Afghanistan, 41, 114; Champigny manifesto, 38; electoralism, 20–1; experience of government, 29–30; Gaullists, 17, 38; Mitterand, 132–6; Party Congresses, 39, 41; presidential election, 22–4; Socialist party, *see* Socialist-Communist Alliance *and* Union of the Left; Soviet Union, 18
concertation, la, 49
Conféderation française démocratique du Travail, 36, 46
CGT, 34
Convention des institutions républicaines, 30, 35
Coty, René, 123, 124
Council of Ministers, 92, 98
Couve de Murville, Maurice, 8, 70, 100
'Crise de régime, la', 13
Czechoslovakia, 71, 109

Debré, Michel: Czechoslovakia, 71; defence, 112, 117; Europe, 21, 79, 91, 98; Gaullist party, 50, 52; Mirages, 75; Pompidou, 9; resignation, 16
decolonization, 4
defence: attitudes after Afghanistan, 111–19; and policy of Giscard d'Estaing, 119–20; reorganization of, 107–8; strategy, 108–11
défense tous azimuts, 73
de Gaulle, General: Algeria, 1–2; definition of presidential role, 125; death, 9, 16; domestic policy, 68; educational background, 138; foreign policy, 9, 68–9, 119; in power, 1–9; RPF, 47
'democratic centralism', 36, 41
Démocratie française, 63, 95, 120
Denmark, 101
détente, 4, 71, 109, 115
Dialogue Nord-Sud, 116
Duhamel, Alain, 22, 60, 64–5, 76, 138, 140
Duverger, Maurice, 42, 124, 133

educational reform, 11
electoralism: development of, 15–19; effects of, 25–6; examples of, 20–5
electoral law (1962), 18, 24
Ellenstein, Jean, 41
energy crisis, the, 77–80
Euratom, 72
'Eurocommunism', 18, 40, 114
European Assembly, 21–2, 49, 86, 97–8, 103
European Commission, 92
European Conference on Security and Co-operation, 72
European Council, 83, 93, 97
European Court, 92
European Defence Community, 108
European Economic Community (EEC): British entry, 9, 70, 79–81, 87, 93–4, 102; European integration, 70; future of, 12, 94–7, 103–5; in Gaullist era, 9, 11, 12; Greece, Portugal and Spain, 97, 100–1; and oil crisis, 79–80; summit conference, 82–3
European monetary fund, 103

European union, 89–94

Faure, Edgar, 62
Fauvet, Jacques, 7, 42–3
Fifth Republic, 1, 3, 19, 27, 47, 138, 140
Fontaine, André, 22, 79, 81, 88, 96, 115
Fouchet plans, 93, 98
Fourcade, Jean-Pierre, 56, 57
Fourth Republic, 1, 3, 25, 27, 58, 74, 137–8
Frears, J. R., x, 48

Gambetta, Léon, 122
Garaud, Marie-France, 116, 135, 139
Gaullism, 51–2, 62, 67
Gaullistes de gauche, 9
Gaullist party: and Communists, 27; after de Gaulle, 6, 11; and fringe groups, 51; and general election 1978, 15; and Giscard d'Estaing, 10, 11; and Giscardians, 49–59; history of, 47–9; leadership and organization of, 50–1; philosophy of, 51–2; and UDF, 28
general elections: 1967, 6, 10; 1968, 7, 10; 1973, 10, 15, 17, 28, 34, 35; 1978, 15, 22, 28, 58
Geneva conference (1961), 72–3
Germany, relations with, 37–8, 73, 87–8, 106–8
Giscard d'Estaing, Valéry: bureaucracy, 136–7; Centrism, 55; defence, 119–20; educational background, 138; electoralism, 23, 25; Europe, 86–105; foreign policy initiatives, 82–5; Gaullists, 10, 11–12, 49–67; Independent Republicans, 47; presidential style, 143
Giscardians, 17, 20, 49–59
Giscardism, 61–7, 112
Government and Politics of France, x
Government Programme of the Socialist Party, 31, 33
gouvernement d'Assemblé, 123
Grandval, Gilbert, 50, 52
Great Britain: entry of to EEC, *see* European Economic Community; political scene in, compared France, 25, 29; relations with, 87–9
Greece, 100
Grosser, Alfred, 89, 96
Guardian, 97
Guichard, Olivier, 50

Hamon, Léo, 44
Henderson, Arthur, 85
Hernu, Charles, 32, 110
'historic compromise, the', 39, 41

immobilisme, 27
Independent Republicans, 28, 47, 48, 54
International Socialist Conference (1950), 29
Ireland, 101
Israel, 74–5

Jobert, Michel, 77, 78, 81, 91, 116
Joll, James, 84
Jospin, Lionel, 42, 43, 114
Juillet, Pierre, 116

Kissinger, Henry, 77, 79

La VIe République et le Régime présidentiel, 124

Laurens, André, 21
Lebrun, President, 122
Lecanuet, Jean, 57, 60, 61, 95
left, the: constitutional problems for, 34–5; future of, 44–6
'left', use of word, 28–9
Lejeune, Max, 58
Le Matin Dimanche, 22
Le Monde, 21, 22, 37, 43, 78, 81, 88, 124
Le Nouveau Siècle, 110
Lévy, Paul, 96
L'Express, 96
L'Humanité, 20
Libya, 75–6, 117
Livre blanc de la défense, 112
lois de programme, 107–8
Luxembourg Agreement, 82–3, 92

McFadzean, Frank, 79
Maire, Edmond, 20
Majorité, la, 48
Marchais, Georges, 21, 23, 32–4, 37–42
Marquand, David, 99, 100
Marxism, 28–9
Mémoires, 5
Méry, General Guy, 110
Messmer plan, 111
Middle East, 74–5, 119
Mirages, sale of, 117–18
Mitterand, François: advisers, 139; autogestion, 36; CIR, 35; 1974 election, 17; 1981 election, 22–4, 41, 59; Europeanism, 99; Jobert, 78; presidential image, 144–5; problems of as president, 130–6; Socialist programme, 32, 45; Tindemans report, 91
Mollet, Guy, 17, 36, 46
Mouvement démocrate socialiste de France, 58

Mouvement des Démocrates, 116
Mouvement républicain populaire (MRP), 66
Mutual and balanced force reductions (MBFR), 72

Nasser, President, 74
National Assembly, the, and the president, 19, 123, 127, 129, 130
national independence, Gaullist policy of, 52, 63, 77, 109–10
Neuwirth, Lucien, 53
North Atlantic Treaty Organization (NATO), 10, 11, 37, 69, 73, 106, 112
nuclear power, 4, 11, 69, 72, 106–11

oil crisis, the, 11, 77–80
Ornano, Michel d', 66
Ortoli, Xavier, 79
Ostpolitik, 73

Pakistan, 118
participation, Gaullist policy of, 51–2
Parti républicain, 57
Parti socialiste unifié, 36
'peace' and 'presence' policy, 74–7
Perspectives et réalités, 56, 57
'petite phrase', the, 33, 34
Peyrefitte, Alain, 94, 95, 96
Pfister, Thierry, 37
Pluto missiles, 110
Political Parties and Elections in the Fifth Republic, x
Pompidolisme, 8, 9, 51
Pompidou, Georges: British entry to EEC, 80–1; death, 9; defence, 117, 119; educational background, 138; five-year plans,

3; foreign policy, 71, 73, 74–7;
Pompidolisme, 8, 9;
presidential image, 142;
resignation, 16
Poniatowski, Michel, 20, 66, 112
Pontillon, Robert, 96, 113
Poperen, Jean, 113
Portugal, 102–3
Potsdam, 5
Poujadist movement, 66–7
Prélot, Marcel, 51
President, the: constitutional powers, problems of, 128–30; in the Fifth Republic, 124–7; and foreign policy, 117; legal status of, 19; and new septennate, 130–3; role of, 12–13; and technocracy, 136–42; in Third and Fourth Republics, 122–3
presidential elections: freak candidates in, 24–5; and general elections, 19; and 1962 referendum, 2–3, 18, 24; 1965, 3, 5, 6, 15, 30; 1969, 15; 1974, 15, 16, 17, 95; 1981, 22–4, 28, 34, 35, 45, 59–61, 111
presidential image, the, 142–5
presidential mandate, reduction of, 133
Programme for a Democratic Government of Popular Union, 31, 33
Projet de société, 114
proportional representation, 133, 134, 141

Quebec, 71

Radical party, 48, 57, 62
Ramadier, Paul, 136
Rassemblement du Peuple Français, 47
Rassemblement pour la République (RPR), 54
referenda, 2, 7, 8, 80, 128–9
regional administration, 11
Républicains indépendants, 16
Republican party, the, 66
République giscardienne, 60, 139
Revel, Jean-François, 131
Rey, Jean, 22
right, the, history of, 47–9
Rocard, Michel, 36, 40, 41, 46, 115
Rome treaty, 10

Sadat, President Anwar, 76
Sanctuarisation du territoire national, la, 113
Sanguinetti, Alexandre, 53
Sauver L'Europe, 96
scandals, 20
Schmidt, Helmut, 87
Servan-Schreiber, Jean-Jacques, 58, 60
Six Day War, 75
Soames, Sir Christopher, 81
Socialist Clubs, 46
Socialist-Communist alliance, 16–18, 28, 35
Socialist Congress (1969), 30–1
Socialist Conventions, 40, 43, 113
Socialist Manifesto, 45, 129, 132
Socialist party: Communist party, *see* Socialist-Communist Alliance *and* Union of the Left; defence, 113; electoralism, 18–22; experience of government, 29–30; Giscardians, 17–18, 20; internal reorganization, 35
Socialist Project, 35, 45, 132, 135
sondages, 14
Soviet Union, relations with, 4–5, 39, 40, 41, 72, 109, 111–19
Spain, 102–3

Stoetzel, Jean, 14
Strategic Arms Limitation Treaty (SALT), 72
student revolution (1968), 7, 72
Suez, 74

The Times, 75, 77, 91, 135
Third Republic, 27, 122
Time, 75, 87
Tindemans report, 89–91
Tindemans, Léo, 89, 99
Todd, Olivier, 96
Treaty of Accession, 82

Union des démocrates pour la République (UDR), 54
Union du peuple de France, 41
Union for French Democracy (UDF), 15, 22, 28, 48, 57–67, 112
Union of the Left, 17–18, 30–40, 42–3
Union pour la nouvelle République (UNR), 47
United Nations, 72
United States, relations with, 5, 77–9

Veil, Simone, 21, 22
Viansson-Ponté, Pierre, 80, 124
Vietnam, 74

Watt, David, 135
Wilson, Sir Harold, 84, 90
Wright, Vincent, x

Yalta, 5